So You've Finished Writing.

Now What?

A beginner's guide to getting your words out there.

by
Fay Rowland

© Fay Rowland 2021

The right of Fay Rowland to be identified as the author of this work is asserted in accordance with the Copyright, Designs and Patents Act 1988.

All rights reserved.

No part of this publication may be reproduced, stored in or introduced into a retrieval system, or transmitted in any form, or by any means (electronic, mechanical, photocopying, recording or otherwise) without the prior written permission of the author. Copies must not be sold, deposited or otherwise distributed.

Visit the author's website at www.fayrowland.co.uk

Typeset at Attic Studios, England in Calibri & Lucida Bright

Published by Thomas Salt Books
ISBN: 978-1-915150-00-4

Contents

From the Author	2
What this book is about	3
Part A — Editing	**5**
Stages of Editing	6
Who, Me?	17
Checklist	20
Part B — Getting Your Words Out There	**29**
Traditional Publishing	30
Author-Funded	35
Hybrid Publishing	40
Indie Publishing	44
Magazines and Newspapers	50
Academic Press	54
Blogging	58
Social Publishing	62
Competitions	66
Part C — Glossary	**69**
The Stuff at the Back	**119**

With Thanks

To Mrs Clarke, English teacher at Homelands School, Derby.

> Aged 11 or so, I asked Mrs Clarke if she had any books I could read.
>
> I'm a teacher myself now, so I can imagine the delight that spread over her face as she showed me the store cupboard of books left over from grammar school days.
>
> She started me with Jane Eyre, still a favourite, and I worked my way through the cupboard over the next few years.
>
> My enduring thanks, Mrs Clarke, for sharing your enthusiasm. And I always liked your pinafore dresses.

To the Association of Christian Writers for their kind support, advice and helpful comments, and for reminding me that God's generous mercy and forgiveness apply even to really horrible first drafts.

To Dwagony, because I always have her in my books even though she is no help whatsoever.

Oh, and my kids, I suppose.

Reviewers Say...

Deserves a place on every writer's desk.

Full of the honest wisdom of experience.

"I can't commend this book enough, particularly to those new to writing. I anticipated it would be merely factual and thus very dry. How wrong can one be? Wonderfully well researched, this comprehensive and detailed guide is full of humour, honest personal experiences and great metaphors, an invaluable reference companion that deserves a place on every writer's desk."

Howard Webber – Award-winning author

"This is a really encouraging and readable guide for those who are new to writing and publishing. It's full of the honest wisdom of experience as well as expertise, and the light-hearted style makes it feel like welcome advice from a friend. There are questions to work through and a review of each of the main forms of publishing, while the fulsome glossary provides a really useful reference guide to key terms and ideas."

Ally Barrett – Author and Chaplain, St Catharine's College, Cambridge.

From the Author

Most writers find people ask them questions like *'My friend / father-in-law / sister's next-door neighbour's nephew has written something. How should they get it published?'*

The last time this happened to me, it was by text message. A text is too small for such an answer, so I started replying by email. I found an email was too small as well, so I crafted my reply as a document.

Other people wanted to read the document and commented things like *I'd like a section on editing,* and *How about a glossary?* And so the document grew and grew and finally became this book.

This is not one of those *'follow my 10-step programme and I guarantee you'll have a best-seller by Christmas'* books. Hopefully, it's full of useful advice and helpful hints, but I am not claiming to be a publishing guru (and it always takes longer than you think).

I am a writer who has experience of several aspects of publishing, both from the inside and the outside. I also have knowledgeable friends whose brains I have picked. So this book is for those of you who can't ask your aunt's neighbour's sister's friend for help.

I hope you find it useful, and I hope you get your words out there.

Blessings,

Fay

What This Book is About

You've finished writing[1]. Awesome! Well done. Have a cup of tea and a choccy biccy.

Now what?

Are you going to leave it languishing on a hard drive, or are you going to put it out there, where people can read it?

Are you going to abandon it to a drawer, festering in the dark for fear of rejection, or allow it to flourish and blossom in the light of day?

Are you going to keep it cowering and shivering like a fledgling on the edge of the nest box, or will you shove it over the brink and watch it spiral pathetically downwards, tiny wings flailing and ...[2]

Ummn ...

OK, that last metaphor didn't work too well.

Never mind. You get the idea. What are you going to do with your writing?

That's what this book is about.

---

[1] 'Finished', of course, includes edited, left it for a while, edited some more, added a new bit, taken it out, edited again, tweaked that section that didn't really work, sent it to **Beta Readers**, got depressed 'cos someone didn't like the ending, changed the ending (but only after sulking for six months), had an existential crisis and nearly thrown the whole thing in the bin, etc.

[2] Obviously, nothing bad happens to the baby bird. It, err, gets picked up by a kindly firefighter and replaced in its nest box, or something.

You have several options for the 'Now What?' depending on your intended audience, how much time and money you are willing to spend, how 'techy' you are, and how much moolah you hope to earn.[3]

Part A of this book is all about editing because, like Jaws, just when you thought it was safe to press 'send' ...[4]

Part B gives you a brief(ish) guide to the main ways to get your lovely words into the hands of people who want to read them. Each method has its own chapter and includes star[5] ratings for aspects such as how likely it is to happen, how much hassle it is, and how long it'll take.

After the ratings, I expand on each heading and finish with a 'How To' section.

Part C is the **Glossary**, which explains all the words in bold type. Following that is The Stuff at the Back (i.e., the **Back Matter**), including my other publications. Do feel free to buy them all.

So, is your chickling ready to be shoved out of the nest box?

---

[3] Spoiler: unless you're J. K. Rowling, take your estimate and divide by 100.

[4] The editing process usually results in fewer lost limbs, however.

[5] 'Book' ratings, actually.

Part A

Editing

My dad's advice on watering a lawn was *do it until you think you've done it too much, then do it some more.* The same applies to editing.[6]

Don't skimp on this stage. You can expect to spend at least as long editing a project as you spent writing it.

Here, I explain the different stages of editing. I discuss who might do these edits, and give you a handy checklist to guide you through the marathon that is the editing process.

Deep breath, here we go.

---

[6] Also to Victorian gothic architecture.

Stages of Editing

There are several steps between a first draft and the finished item. Depending on the length and type of your writing you may not need all of them, or you may have to repeat some several times.

The editing process starts with a broad view and zooms in on smaller and smaller details, ending with the microscopic nit-picking of proof readers.

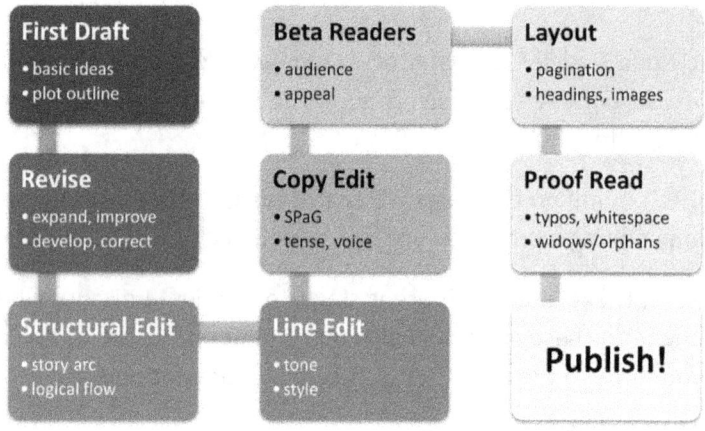

This diagram shows all the possible stages, but don't be put off; remember that you might not need them all.

On the other hand, you might need to loop back to an earlier step, like in snakes and ladders. In fact, you almost certainly will. But I have not shown that because it would make the diagram look like a plate of spaghetti.

You may be able to combine some stages, but it's usually easier to concentrate on one thing at a time. Of course, if you spot a typo or change of tense during a structural read-through, by all means change it or mark it for correction. But you have a better view of the landscape if you are not actively looking for daisies.

Should You Self-edit?

Yes.

And no.

Allow me to explain:

You've checked something ten times and you're absolutely sure it's perfect, so you hit 'send' and sit back.

And then you see the glaring typo on page 2.

Irritating, isn't it? But we've all done it. No editor is perfect. Even professional editors will say they aim to pick up 90% of errors, not 100%.

So think of editors as leaky umbrellas. Each layer is imperfect, but put several together and you're as dry as a Bond martini.

So yes, you should definitely edit your own work, but don't be the *only* one who does it.

First Draft

This stage is quick and dirty – get your ideas on the page with a rough outline of where you start, where you finish, and how you get from one to the other. Just get it down on the page.

Drafts can come together speedily if the ideas are flowing. When a train from Manchester to London was delayed by four hours, the result was the first draft of *Harry Potter*.

Don't worry about typos. Don't worry about slips. Don't worry about run-on sentences or split infinitives. This is the place for the somewhat dubious adage of 'write drunk, edit sober'.[7] And don't even *think* about word count.

> Don't cross out. Don't worry about spelling, punctuation, grammar. Lose control. Don't think. Don't get logical. Go for the jugular.
> — *Natalie Goldberg*

Your first draft is a load of dung? That's fine. Dung makes excellent fertiliser.

Revise

It's pretty much impossible to write something that's ready to publish on the first draft, so go through it all again. And again. Revisions are where those good ideas become a great reality.

Roald Dahl's *Matilda* had a total rewrite to become the diminutive heroine we know today. In the first draft, she was a horrible child who used her powers unkindly, and Dahl disliked the character he had created.

---

[7] My fine, upstanding editor notes that it is not strictly necessary to be drunk in order to write, although Edgar Allan Poe sounds like he was.

> *I got it wrong. I'd spent six or eight or nine months writing it and right when I'd finished ... it just wasn't right ... So I started the whole book again and rewrote every word.*
> — Roald Dahl

Everything can be improved with a rewrite (J.K. Rowling reputedly rewrote the opening chapter of *Harry Potter and the Philosopher's Stone* fifteen times!), and you would not want to send your second best out, would you?

Structural Edit

Once you have completed your story, article, or guide to the cheese-makers of Renfrewshire, the first major edit is called structural, developmental or content editing. This stands back and takes a long view, surveying the overall flow and structure of the piece.

For works of fiction, it looks at the storyline as a whole and checks for plot holes and loose ends. It considers character development, major and minor story arcs, and whether any sub-plot adds to or distracts from the main narrative.

Structural editing also looks at the pace – does this section drag or is another part too skimpy and needs fleshing out?

For non-fiction pieces, a structural edit looks at the logical flow of ideas: does A lead to B, and have you shown a progression of thought? Do you establish facts before you use them?

It's important to do this edit early in the process. There is no point spending weeks copy editing a section of dialogue that you are going to delete in a structural re-jig.

This is also the time to think about your Unique Selling Point. Why would anyone buy your book over someone else's? Sadly, in this age of a million books a minute,[8] no USP means no sale. Teenage romance? Nah. Teenage *vampire* romance? Now you're talking.

Following a structural edit, you might rearrange, add, delete, reduce or expand sections.[9] Be sure to repeat the process afterwards, because changing even small things can have large effects – think how differently *Romeo and Juliet* would have ended had the apothecary's been closed that day.

Questions to ask

- Do you repeat ideas anywhere?
- Are the ideas in the right order?
- Are your facts backed up with data or quotations where needed?
- Does the plot tie up nicely?
- Is the pacing right?
- Are all **Narrative Arcs** complete?
- Do you have a **USP**?

Line Edit

Line editing is often used interchangeably with copy editing and the two stages can be combined. A line editor considers the work at paragraph and sentence level (i.e., line by line). Is the sentence clear and powerful? Does it have the right tone for the readership (formal / chatty / poetic etc.) Does it have

---

[8] OK, slight exaggeration. Book sales in the UK in 2020 were just shy of 400 books a minute. But that still adds up to over 200 million in the UK alone. Which is quite a lot of books.

[9] This whole section is the result of a structural edit after **Beta Readers** commented that they'd like more information on editing.

the correct reading age for your audience – and that does not apply only to children!

Would it have been at all possible, do you think, to have conveyed the identical sense of meaning with fewer and simpler words, that is to say, with a smaller number of subordinate clauses, less jargon, a less-convoluted sentence structure and, to summarise, in a more succinct and enticing manner?

In writing, less is almost always better.[10]

Check if you use a favourite phrase repetitively. Is your hero constantly tossing their tousled hair from their eyes? Does every second paragraph start with 'But then'? Or are you just using 'just' too much? (That one is my pet foible.) English is the biggest language in the world for a reason: we have a heck of a lot of synonyms. So use them!

You will probably go through this process several times, and it's not time wasted. This is the stage that will change your grey, matte-finish text into something with the colour, depth and texture of a Vivienne Westwood[11] couture collection.

> *I love to rewrite. I especially like to cut: to press the DELETE key and see an unnecessary word or phrase or sentence vanish into the electricity. I like to replace a humdrum word with one that has more precision or color ... I like to rephrase a drab sentence to give it a more pleasing rhythm or a more graceful musical line.*
> — William Zinsser

---

[10] The opposite is true with chocolate.

[11] Or Simone Rocha if that dates me.

Questions to ask

- Are the tone and style right for the audience?
- Does each paragraph contain only one topic?
- Can you replace weak verbs and adjectives with stronger ones?
- Does the text 'flow'?

Copy Edit

This focuses on the word-level of editing and checks the SPaG: Spelling, Punctuation and Grammar. It is often mistakenly called proof reading (which comes later).

You should carefully check any required **Style Guides** to make sure that you stick to the conventions and house style. No publisher wants to change all your double quotes into single quotes or swap American spellings to British.

You should have been careful to maintain a consistent tense throughout, and didn't change from present to past halfway through. The editor should also ensure that the text does not suddenly swap to the third person from the second.[12]

If you use **References**, now is the time to check that they refer to the right thing and are formatted correctly. I know it's a huge pain in the bum, but it really does need doing. Sorry.

This is also the place for fact-checking, both in fiction and non-fiction. Could your Edwardian hero have placed that telephone call without contacting the operator?[13]

---

[12] Arghh! I hate that paragraph, and it was so hard to write.

[13] Nope. The first UK direct-dial call was in 1958, made by Her Majesty QEII. Before that, the operator could have listened in and heard the whole dastardly plan.

Questions to ask

- SPaG – are spelling, punctuation and grammar correct and in accordance with any **Style Guide**?
- Are references correct and properly formatted?
- Do you need to check any facts?
- Are headings and sub-headings consistently capitalised?
- Have you formatted numbers consistently?

Beta Readers

You are the alpha reader, and when you have got to a stage when you are ready for some customer feedback, you need beta readers. This stage could easily go earlier, after the structural edit, for example, but certainly no later than here.

Choose friends, relatives or other writers who match your intended audience, and who can be trusted to be honest. It's nice to have encouragement, but you also need to check that you're headed in the right direction. Alongside "Well done. It's fab!" we also need to hear "How come Mr Parkin knew about the baby in chapter 3 but he didn't in chapter 5?"

Comments from beta readers can result in a major rebuilding project, in which case you loop back up to the structural edit stage and go through it all again (sigh).

> *The only kind of writing is rewriting.*
> — Ernest Hemingway

Layout

When you are quite sure that all the words are in their final order you are ready for layout. There should be no major changes from this point, only the brushing away of a stray hair, or the light powdering of a shiny nose.

Layout puts your words into their place on the page. If you are publishing electronically, you may need no layout other than titles. With other methods, such as magazines and traditional book publishing, layout is done for you, so you can skip over this section. However, if you are indie publishing or using a commercial printer, you will need to construct the inside of the book, neatly align images and diagrams, choose heading styles, check pagination, and assemble the **Front** and **Back Matter**.

This is a subject that can fill a whole book by itself, so I will merely say, 'simpler is better'. No more than two typefaces (one for the body text, one for headings). Keep illustrations and design elements consistent, leave plenty of **Whitespace**, and if in doubt, employ a professional.

Proof Read

The final version of your writing, just before it is printed, is called a proof,[14] and reading the proof is, amazingly, called proof reading.

In this very final stage of the process, you are looking for errors introduced in the layout process and catching anything missed in earlier stages. Changes at this stage should be very, very small indeed. Hopefully, non-existent.

You should check heading and image **Alignment**, pagination (important pages, such as new chapters, are usually on the right) and consistency in page design.

Look out for **Widows and Orphans**, awkward line breaks and **Rivers** of whitespace. Make sure that the pages listed in the contents are what they should be, and that the title page is correct.

---

[14] Proof here means test, as in 'the proof of the pudding is in the eating'.

Sadly, the habit of humans to see what they expect means that it's nigh impossible to proof your own work. By all means do the first pass, but always get a fresh pair of eyes.[15] See the sections below for some useful tips.

This is also the stage at which you may be writing the **Blurb**, **Logline**, publicity materials etc, if you have not done so already. You might also be checking the cover artwork and author info, making sure it matches with the inside, and deciding the price and launch date. It really is nearly there![16]

Questions to ask

- Are the typefaces and font sizes correct?
- Are the sub-headings of the right level?
- Is the contents page correct?
- Are there any widows or orphans?
- Are headers and footers properly aligned?
- Are images in the right places and correctly captioned?
- Are there any awkward hyphenations?
- Are there unsightly rivers of whitespace?
- Are the paragraphs correctly spaced, with consistent **Leading** above and below headings?
- Do important pages appear on the right?

Publish

Phew! You've finished. Sit back relax and put your feet up.

---

[15] I mean get someone else to look over it. Not *literally* get new eyes. Not sure where you'd get them from, anyway. Not sure I want to know.

[16] Exciting, innit?

Nah, only kidding. Now you can start marketing[17], converting to **eBook**[18] and clawing your way up those best-seller charts.

And have you thought about a sequel?

---

[17] Ideally, you started this quite a while ago.

[18] Ditto.

Who, Me?

Yes, you. You are your first editor. But even the best barber can't cut his own hair, so while you should do the first edits yourself, you will need other eyes at some stage in the process.

There are three people or groups of people who can do the various stages of editing. Which you'll choose is dependent on the length and importance of the writing, your expertise and preferences and, if you will pardon my vulgarity, money.

Most successful indie-published authors say that if you pay for anything, pay for professional editing and cover design. I second that, but you need to balance costs and benefits. A good edit is essential to any book, but spending £500 to gain five extra sales is probably not worth it.

You

You should be the first port-of-call in most editing jobs. You should do the first structural edit, the first copy edit, the first proof read.

In some cases that will be all that is needed. The thank-you letter to Great Aunt Mabel for her hand-knitted jumper with assorted winter wildlife in jaunty Santa hats probably does not need checking over by a professional copy editor. Your 1,000-page *magnum opus* probably does.[19]

You can improve your editing skills with the tips below, and you can take copy-editing courses to reduce the amount of work you need to pay someone else to do.

---

[19] And probably needs shortening, too. See text attached to footnote 10.

Non-professionals

The second stop on your journey might be well-read friends, family, or members of your local writers' group.

Make sure that they would feel happy telling you about any errors they find, and that you would be OK hearing it. You are not looking for a pat on the back at this stage.

Writers' groups can be a great way to find people who will review each other's work on a mutual back-scratching basis.

If you are not confident with your standard of English, don't let that put you off writing. Find a friend who will go through your text with you and swap out the Denglish[20] for something more idiomatic. This will save time and expense at the professional editing stage.

Professionals

If you can afford one, hiring a professional editor is one of the best investments you can make. (The other is a professional cover designer.) Traditional publishing houses, newspapers and magazines employ their own editors, but they will still appreciate having to do as little work as possible on your manuscript, so a professional edit will maximise your chances of success.

---

[20] The language written by my Danish friend. All power to his elbow, I say. I certainly could not write a novel in my second language!

Handy Hints for Editing

Leave it
Hide it under a pile of books. Stuff it down the back of the sofa. Put it in a pillowcase and sleep on it.[21] Seriously, this is my best bit of advice. You'll be amazed how much more you will see when you come back to your manuscript after a break.

> *There's no page of prose in existence that its author can't improve after it's been in a drawer for a week.*
> *— Charles Finch*

Different format
Print it out on paper, resize the page, or use a different font to help you dig those sneaky little typos from their hiding places.

Out loud
OK, I realise that you can't do this in an office, but reading out out loud is a great way to notice awkward phrases, difficult-to-follow sentences and missing or repeated words. (Did you spot it?) It can help you to hear the rhythm of your text, whether it lilts and flows, or stumbles and crashes.

Tapping / backwards
Tapping each word with a pencil, or reading lines backwards, makes you look at the words separately, rather than scanning ahead as we usually do when reading.

---

[21] However, do *not* put it in a capacious handbag and leave it in the cloakroom of one of London's larger railway stations. Victoria. The Brighton line. (With apologies to Oscar Wilde.)

Checklist

Here are some common bugbears of editors and publishers.

If you have not yet made all the mistakes below, please be patient. It takes time to gather such an inauspicious litany of twerpdom, but it will come. Oh yes, it will come.

Show, Don't Tell

I'm guessing you've heard this one before, but just in case you haven't:

> *Shona was feeling hungry and tired. She walked over to Naz and asked for food. Naz was ashamed to admit that he did not have any food left.*

or

> *Shona punched her complaining stomach and trudged over to Naz's food bar.*
>
> *"What have you got?" she asked. "Anything will do. As long as it's stodgy. And quick."*
>
> *Naz watched the last shift of workers leave. Mess all over his tables. More cleaning. He glanced at Shona and then at his scraped-out serving dishes.*
>
> *"Ummn," he said and fiddled with his apron. But he didn't finish.*

The second example does not *tell* us that Shona is hungry, nor that Naz has run out of food and is embarrassed, but we certainly know, and we're in the room with them. Can you smell the left-over curry?

Flabby Prose

When I edited a small community magazine, I found I could cut a quarter of the words from most submitted articles without losing any meaning. As writers, we should attempt to do this cutting before the text leaves our hands.

If I'm writing commissioned pieces, I don't worry about word count to start with. I say all I want to say, and then I grab my machete and slash those flabby 3,000 words down to the svelte 2,000 I will submit. The same ruthless removal of dead material applies to all genres. If you have three sentences describing your hero's clothing, choose the best two. You don't need to sacrifice content, only words.

Don't think of it as losing your precious work; think of it as removing gangrene.[22] Cut! Cut! Cut!

Sentence Length

This sentence is six words long. This one is the same length. There's nothing wrong with six words. Six words make a fine sentence. But writing like this sounds boring. It's like a block of flats. Each one is exactly the same. There is no variation or dynamic.

But now let's try something different: something new, something exciting, something ... brave! You with me? Let's dare to use longer sentences with complex structures that draw the reader along your train of thought. Let's use shorter ones. Even sentence fragments.

So much more interesting, don't you agree?

---

[22] If that's a bit yukky, try a sculptor removing all the stone that doesn't look like a lion.

Run-on Sentences / Comma Splice

While we're on the subject of sentences, make sure that each one is one, not two. A run-on sentence is two sentences smushed into one, it's like a bendy bus – two busses connected with a joint between.[23]

That joint is known as a comma splice and is considered bad style. Either use a full stop to make two sentences, join them with a semi-colon, or make one into a subordinate clause.

SPaG

Whether it is your **Query Letter** or the first chapter that you submit if it is full of run-on sentences lacking in punctuation or had grammatical error any reader is going to assume that the rest of the text is the same and lazy presentation usually means lazy writing to.

Go back and do a thorough copyedit, concentrating of the spelling, punctuation and grammar.[24]

Uncertain Language

Writing that is full of *might*, *seems to* and *could possibly*, might seem to be, possibly, uncertain of what it is saying.

Unless these phrases are strictly needed, you should replace them with more definite language.

---

[23] This was one, just there.

[24] How many errors can you spot in this entry? I counted 11.

To Be or Not?

If you have a lot of sentences that feature 'to be' helper verbs, consider changing the main verb to something stronger.

For example:

> *In order to be a first-class writer, you have to be a first-class editor, too.*

or

> *First-class writers are first-class editors, too.*

Shorter, clearer and snappier.

Additional Adverbs

Adding adverbs to everything might be a sign that you need better verbs.

For example:

> *Martin dressed hurriedly then walked quickly to the door and loudly asked, "Is Mr Farthing there?"*

or

> *Martin threw on his clothes and raced to the door. "Is Mr Farthing there?" he demanded.*

Use interesting verbs so that your hero doesn't have to sit on a chair when they could flop, drape or perch there instead.

The only exception to this is 'said'. By all means have your hero croon, cheer or plead occasionally, but only occasionally. It is tiring to read twenty different verbs in every conversation, so unless there is a reason to use a different verb, go with 'said'.

Cliché

As blind as a bat? Boring. One might even say 'as dull as ditch water', were that not boring too. How about 'as dull as a March[25] morning', or 'as dull as canteen soup'?

But it's not just similes; stories can be cliché as well. Does your gritty, steel-eyed hero become softened by a curly-haired kid and walk into the sunset with said curly-haired kid's mother?

Hmmn. Didn't I see that in a perfume advert last week?

Filler Words

Well, these are the words we add when speaking, you see, to give our brains time to catch up. They also sneak into our writing. Look for words that can be removed from a sentence without changing its meaning, such as 'that', 'very' and 'even'.

For example:

> *With the moon shining even and bright, Marcus could even see his own breath as he stood watching, even hoping, for the train to arrive, even though it was not due for an hour or even more.*

Irritating, isn't it? The first one is OK, that's not a filler, but the others – death to them!

> *With the moon shining even and bright, Marcus could see his breath as he stood watching, hoping, for the train to arrive, although it was not due for an hour or more.*

Much better.

---

[25] I live in the UK. Feel free to substitute any month.

Pesky Pronouns

Make sure that each pronoun clearly refers to the right noun. As an example of poor practice, here is a genuine sign from outside a building in London.

> *Please do not chain your bicycle to these railings as they will be removed.*

I wonder how many sets of railing they've got through.

Dangling Modifiers

Similarly, make sure that descriptive phrases refer to the right noun.

> *The camel carried Janet towards the pyramids, flicking hair out of her eyes with manicured fingers.*

Really? The camel?

Not Really Very Nice

These are weak adjectives. We can do better than that.

For example:

> *That is a really very nice dress.*

or

> *That is a stylish / awesome / gorgeous / flattering / expensive-looking / sock-'em-in-the-eyeballs dress.*

Passive Voice

Passive voice is needed when you do not wish to, or cannot, specify who does the verb (like at the start of this sentence). But where the actor is known, it is better to use the active voice.

For example:

  The mat was sat upon by the cat.

or

  The cat sat on the mat.

Jar-gone

If you are writing for a specialist audience who will understand that 'toad'[26] refers to a small vehicle pulled behind a motorhome, or that 'LBJ'[27] means a small, dun-coloured bird of indeterminate brand then fine, use the jargon. Otherwise, explain it either by writing it out fully at the first occurrence, by using **Footnotes** or by providing a **Glossary**.

If you are writing for a general audience, try to avoid jargon because it produces an 'in' group of people who understand it and, consequently, an 'out' group.

Having said that, most people prefer to write DNA instead of deoxyribonucleic acid.[28]

---

[26] Because it's towed – gettit?

[27] Little Brown Job. Probably a female house sparrow, but who knows?

[28] And BAPTA instead of 1,2-bis(2-aminophenoxy)ethane-N,N,N',N'-tetraacetic acid?

Are We Nearly There Yet?

How many emails have you sent and then had to send again this time *with* the attachment? Yup, me too. There is nothing that does not benefit from revision.

Submitting your work before you have finished editing is like eating green bananas; you can, I guess, but it will be so much better later.[29]

Don't be in a hurry to press 'send'. Take your time. Send your writing out looking its best. Polish its shoes, brush its hair and give it a mint in case of bad breath.

> *Writing without revising is the literary equivalent of waltzing gaily out of the house in your underwear.*
> — *Patricia Fuller*

So edit until you think you've done it too much, then edit some more.

Thanks for the advice, Dad.

---

[29] Conversely, cake mixture is often better than the finished cake. Especially if you're a rubbish cook, like me.

Part B

Getting Your Words Out There

Whether you are writing a romantic sci-fi comedy or a how-to guide for nose-hair weaving, there is no 'best' way to publish. Different ways suit different people at different times.

I'll list methods ranging from traditional publishing to various types of **Self-Publishing** (with info on avoiding vanity presses). I'll set out the pros and cons, and rate these features out of 5:

Likely: How likely is it to happen? Pipe dream or realistic?

Low Hassle: How much time and effort will you have to put into the process? Will you need specialist skills?

Cheap: How much will it cost you?

Profitable: How much are you likely to earn? Extremely vague. Don't quote me on this.

Quick: How long does it take to get your words out there?

Distribution: How many people will get to see your writing?

Best for: Who might find this a suitable route?

Traditional Publishing

This is the method everyone thinks of first. The process, according to Hollywood, is:

- You approach one of the big **Publishing Houses** and say, "I've written a fabulous book."
- "That's awesome," they say. "Have some money."
- They produce your beautiful book.
- Prince William, Taylor Swift and The Pope all write gleaming **Endorsements** for the cover.
- Three weeks later, your book lands in bookshops worldwide. **Royalty** cheques slip through your door daily and you never have to work again.

Hmmmn. No, not really. Pretty much every item on that wish list is wrong, despite what happened to Hugh Jackman in *Paperback Hero*.

Nevertheless, a book deal is the dream of most writers.

Ratings

Likely:	📖
Low Hassle:	📖 📖 📖 📖 📖
Cheap:	📖 📖 📖 📖 📖
Profitable:	📖 📖
Quick:	📖
Distribution:	📖 📖 📖 📖 📖
Best for:	Famous people, and authors with a history of writing commercially successful books.

Likely 📖

Not very.

Less than that.[30]

Traditional publishers need to make a profit, so they want books they know they can sell. Most publishers get thousands more **Proposals** than they can accept, so they are very picky and many only accept submissions from **Agents**, not authors.

The most likely response you will get from sending your **Manuscript** to a publisher (especially if you have not followed their **Submission Guidelines**) is silence. The second most likely is a computer-generated "Thank you, but no thanks" **Rejection Slip**. The third most likely is a personally written rejection letter, and the least likely of all is an invitation to send in the rest of the manuscript.

Don't be disheartened by this. It happens to the best of us. Kathryn Stockett's *The Help* gathered 60 rejections over 3½ years, but became 7 million books and an award-winning film.

Rejection does not mean that your work is rubbish, simply that it's not what that publisher is looking for at that time. Make sure your submission package is up to snuff, then try again with a different publisher.

Low Hassle 📖📖📖📖📖

If you are lucky enough to be accepted by a publishing house, you sign a **Contract**, and the publisher takes over from there. They handle all aspects of getting your book ready for market, from editing to illustrations, from design to distribution.

---

[30] Less than that as well.

The upside of this is that it leaves you to get on with writing your next book, safe in the knowledge that everything is in the hands of professionals. The downside is that you lose control of your 'baby'. You may have little say in the decisions, so if you prefer a more hands-on approach, try a different method.

Yet while there are many excellent methods of self-publishing these days, none match the prestige of traditional publishing, nor the access to top editors, designers etc.

Cheap

This method costs the author nothing, either up front or later. Neither agents nor publishers charge for taking your book on.

If you are asked to pay for your book to be published, it's not a traditional publisher.

Profitable

You will be paid royalties, a fixed percentage of the sale price of the book. This is usually disappointingly low, but you must bear in mind that lots of people need to be paid, not only you.

Let's say the **List Price** of your book is £9.99 (the publisher decides this, not you). Bookshops buy it from the publisher for £4.50. (55% **Wholesale Discount** is common.) From this, the publisher covers the cost of printing, pays editors, illustrators and proof readers, and takes some to cover losses on other books. You get what's left, which might be 5% of the sale price.

Yes, that's right. You could make 50p per book.[31] Leave that holiday in The Seychelles for a year or two, perhaps?

---

[31] But 200 million books x 50p makes a lot of dosh if you're Dan Brown.

Quick

In words of one syllable or fewer: no.

If you want your book out by Christmas, forget traditional publishing. It takes a very long time. Even getting a rejection slip can take 3-6 months.

Distribution

Traditional publishers have access to all the major **Bricks-and-Mortar** bookshops, libraries, schools and online retailers. Heck, you might even see your book in the local supermarket. Publishers will often have international and translation rights too, so they can distribute in other countries as appropriate.

No publishing method comes close to the distribution reach of trad publishers, especially **The Big Five/Four** – Harper Collins, Hachette Book Group, Macmillan and Penguin Random House.

Best For …

… established authors, if I'm honest. Or Richard Osman.

If you have a track record of writing books that sell, or a large fan base, traditional publishers are going to take you more seriously than if you've never written before and no one has heard of you.

Sad to say, breaking into traditional publishing is pretty hard for new authors. Sorry.

How To

By all means, try for traditional publishing if you write in a popular **Genre**. Don't be put off by rejections. Try again somewhere else. There are lots of **Niche** publishers besides The Big Five/Four. You can find details in *The Writers' and Artists' Yearbook*, available in libraries or to buy.

Many large publishers also have **Imprints** for particular genres or styles of books such as Ladybird, an imprint of Penguin. One of these may be a better fit for your work.

Find a publisher or imprint that produces the kind of book you write, visit their website and see if they are accepting **Submissions**. If they are not, don't bug them. If they are, look at their **Submission Guidelines** and follow them. *To. The. Nanometre.*

Many traditional publishers work through literary agents who sort the wheat from the chaff for them.[32] So you may need to preface your search with finding an agent.

Write a stellar **Query Letter** – this is likely the only thing an editor will read, so make it good – and send your baby off in a reed basket.

And then wait ...

---

[32] The chaff is used as scripts for Celebrity Love Island.

Author-Funded

This is the opposite of **Traditional Publishing** and your only other option until relatively recently. With the traditional method, the publisher pays for everything and owns all the books, but with author-funded, you pay for everything and own all the books.

Author-funded publishing is a great option for small **Print Runs** and limited distributions: souvenirs, school fundraisers, and books of local walks to raise money for a village defibrillator.

You ask a commercial printer or bookbinder to print your books and deliver them to you. Job done. They may provide simple editorial and layout services, but they do not sell or distribute your books. That's down to you.

A Note on Vanity Publishing

Author-funded is the publishing world's dodgy end of town. There are some companies which exist merely to sell you their services for as much money as possible. These are **Vanity Presses**, and it can be tricky to tell them apart from reputable commercial printers and **Author Services**.

What is vanity publishing?

Vanity publishing is sometimes used as an umbrella term for everything that is not traditional publishing, but this is both inaccurate and unkind. There are many alternatives these days, and many reasons for self-publishing that have nothing to do with pride.

Vanity presses / publishers are scam-merchants who exploit unwary authors. They often masquerade as traditional or hybrid publishers, and their quick acceptance and fulsome praise for your **Manuscript** is

35

nice if you've had a ton of rejection letters, but be aware that the lack of scrutiny comes at two prices:

The first is a literal price. These businesses make their money from authors, not books, and often charge way over the odds.

The second price is quality. Vanity presses don't care if your book sells and have no incentive to produce quality products. Almost no bookshop will stock these self-published books and, sadly, this poor reputation rubs off on the rest of self-publishing.

You are 100% likely to be accepted by a vanity press. If you see an advert for new authors, guaranteeing to publish any book, you would be well advised to turn and walk swiftly in the other direction.

Remember, for every Random House, there is also a bloke in a random house waiting to take your money.

Ratings

Likely: 📖📖📖📖📖
Low Hassle: 📖📖📖
Cheap: 📖
Profitable: 📖📖
Quick: 📖📖📖
Distribution: 📖
Best for: Books that you want to distribute yourself.

Likely 📖📖📖📖📖

Same as booking a restaurant. Provided they've got space, you're in. The printer's job is to print books, not to sell them, so they do not vet manuscripts for quality or saleability.

Commercial printers will print anything you ask them to, and that includes typos and upside-down photos. Don't assume they'll check your work for errors.

Low Hassle 📖📖📖

This gets a mid-range score because, on one hand, it is pretty low hassle. There are no editors to navigate around, no quality checks, no re-writes. You simply give them the manuscript and the money, and they give you the books.

On the other hand, the onus is on you to make sure it is all correct. You are responsible for the content, images, choice of **Font**, even **cover design** and **ISBN**s, and these may be beyond your skillset. In that case, you need to do some speedy learning or hire professionals.

Some commercial printers provide **Author Services**, such as **Editing** and **Layout**. These can be useful, but ask to see samples of work before you pay up and make sure you are only paying for services you want.

Cheap 📖

To quote a certain acid-tongued judge from Strictly Come Dancing, "It's only got a one because I haven't got a zero, darling."

This is the most expensive method. On the plus side, that box of unsold books can make a useful and stylish coffee table.

Profitable 📖📖

You'll be selling these books yourself, so unless you own a bookshop, you'll have a very limited market. It's best to have people order beforehand so you can guarantee to sell all the copies.

Alternatively, you might be printing a promotional book or a giveaway, so making a loss is not a problem.

As a fund-raiser, you will hopefully cover costs and make some pennies for your charity because people will buy a book for a good cause, but if you want to make your living as an author, you might like to try a different route.

Quick 📖📖📖📖

Pretty fast turnaround depending on how busy the printer is. It's definitely a lot faster than traditional publishing.[33]

Distribution 📖

Zilch.
Zero.
Zip.
I think you catch my drift.

But that's fine if you're making a school yearbook to sell to parents. Who cares that Waterstones will never stock it? That was never your aim.

---

[33] But then, apart from the orbit of Neptune, what isn't?

Best For …

… limited-distribution books. A drama society might want souvenir programmes, or a church could produce an illustrated history for its 500-year anniversary. A photographer might make a coffee table book. A public speaker or a poet could have books to sell at the back of the hall.

Also good for charity fund-raisers (but do your sums carefully to make sure you'll cover costs).

How To

Essentially, the process is the same as ordering pizza.[34] You find a company and tell them what to make. You pay the price. They deliver. That's it.

You can often find 'printed by' notices inside the back cover of promotional booklets and local magazines, so that can be a good way to find good-quality printers in your area. If you are happy to do everything online, there are many companies providing print-on-demand services.

However, be wary of unsolicited offers. Reputable printers and publishing houses will not usually approach you, offering to print your book. Vanity presses will.

---

[34] But with fewer choices of crust.

Hybrid Publishing

This is a cross between **Traditional Publishing**, and author-funded. In hybrid publishing, the author pays for some of the books and the publisher funds the rest, and any profits are similarly shared. It's also called **Co-Publishing**.

In this model, the author commits to buying part of the **Print Run** to sell at events or via their **Website**. The rest belong to the publisher who sells via bookshops, either online or **Bricks-and-Mortar**.

Generally, the costs and profits should be split 50-50. You can compare with other publishers to make sure that you're getting a fair deal.

Ratings

Likely: 📖📖📖
Low Hassle: 📖📖📖📖
Cheap: 📖📖
Profitable: 📖📖📖
Quick: 📖📖📖
Distribution: 📖📖📖
Best for: Commercially viable books by lesser-known authors who have some money to invest.

Likely 📖📖📖

Because hybrid publishers do not shoulder as much financial burden as traditional publishers, they can afford to take risks with less-well-known authors. Hybrid publishers want to be sure they can sell their share of the print run, so they will still be picky, but there is more wiggle-room in this model.

Low Hassle 📖📖📖📖

As with a traditional publisher, once you have signed the **Contract**, the publisher takes over. The **Editing**, **Typesetting** etc, are done for you, and all you'll have to do is approve the **Proofs**.

It does not get five stars, however, because you may find it a hassle to sell your copies.

Cheap 📖📖

While certainly not as expensive as funding the whole shebang yourself, hybrid publishing comes at the expensive end of the spectrum. As compensation, of course, you get a large pile of books, which you might have purchased anyway as **Author Copies** from an **Indie Publisher**. So it may come out even.

Do the maths before you sign the contract and work out how many books you will have to sell and at what price before you start making a profit. And watch out for vanity presses in sheep's clothing.

Profitable 📖📖📖

This is Radio 2 territory.[35] You have an initial outlay which you'll have to cover before you make a profit, but you'll have a bundle of discounted books to sell. It depends on how good you are at selling books and how good a discount.

Hybrid publishers pay **Royalties**, (usually at a higher rate than traditional and lower than indie publishers), but you should not rely on this for paying your mortgage.

Quick 📖📖📖

Again, middle of the road. Not as fast as some methods, but faster than others.

Distribution 📖📖📖

Yet again, we're dancing along the dotted line. Hybrid publishers should be able to get your books onto the shelves of mainstream bookshops, but smaller publishers will not have the cachet of **The Big Five/Four**. And you have your share of the print run to sell, which may be a blessing or a curse.

Best For ...

... authors who want the professional look of a publishing house but have got sick of rejection slips. If you don't want the hassle of indie publishing and have some money to invest, then this might be the route for you.

---

[35] Middle of the road.

How To

As with traditional publishers, find one that prints the sort of books you write, check their **Submission Guidelines**, and polish that **Query Letter**.

Google your company and check the books they have printed. Then find those books on Amazon and make sure they are selling. Avoid companies that have lax editorial standards – it might make it easy to get your book out, but at the cost of poor quality.

Be sure to check the details of your contract, particularly how many books you have to buy and at what cost. If either seems unreasonably high, you may have stumbled upon a vanity press by mistake. Go somewhere else.

Indie Publishing

Indie (independent) publishing is the new kid on the self-publishing block. Modern print-on-demand (**POD**) technology means that books can be printed *after* they have been sold, so there is no need for the financial risk of printing 1000 copies that may end up as an eco-alternative to barbeque briquettes.

Print-on-demand technology enables authors to complete the entire publishing process, from first draft through to sales, by themselves. Indie publishing involves the most work, but it also produces the biggest returns per copy.

There is almost no editorial oversight in this method – everything is handled by machines – so people[36] can publish under-edited, sub-standard dross. However, those quickly fall down the search-engine algorithms and good indie-published books can top the bestsellers lists alongside their traditionally-published peers.

Although there are other platforms, such as Kobe and Apple Books, Amazon's Kindle Direct Publishing (**KDP**) is by far the biggest player, selling two-thirds of all **eBooks**, and about half of US paperbacks.

A Note on ISBNs

One of the most common questions people ask when considering indie publishing, is 'Do I need an ISBN?' This is usually followed by 'How do I get one?'

Do I need one?

Maybe. ISBNs are used by publishers, shops and libraries for identifying a particular edition of a book.

---

[36] Not you, obviously.

So if you want these places to know about your book, you'll need an ISBN. But if you intend to give your publication away or distribute it yourself only, you do not need one.

ISBNs do not register you as the author of the work or give copyright protection, nor do they assign you any rights. An ISBN is simply a product identification code.

How do I get one?

Each country has an organisation that dispenses ISBNs. In the UK this is Nielsen, in the US, Bowker. You can buy ISBNs individually, or in packs of 10, 100 or more, and these are registered to you forever. Each separate edition of a book (paperback, hardback, large print, illustrated, eBook, etc.) needs its own ISBN.

Traditional publishers supply ISBNs as part of their package while commercial printers generally do not. Hybrid publishers and indie platforms may offer one either free or for a price.

Ratings

Likely:	📖📖📖📖
Low Hassle:	📖
Cheap:	📖📖📖📖
Profitable:	📖📖📖📖📖
Quick:	📖📖📖📖📖
Distribution:	📖📖📖📖
Best for:	Authors who are confident with the technical nitty-gritty.

Likely 📖📖📖📖

Indie platforms do not take any financial risk by publishing your book, so they do not need to be sure your book will sell before accepting you. This means platforms like **KDP** are very likely to accept your manuscript.

However, this method does not rate 5 stars because the technical know-how required may prove a barrier. Although it does not pass under the beady eye of an **Acquisitions Editor** looking for polished grammar and an inspiring **Story Arc**, your manuscript could be rejected for not having the right **Trim Size** or correctly **Embedded Fonts**. If you don't know (and don't care) what those are, this might not be a good method for you.

Low Hassle 📖

Nope. This is the highest hassle route. But if you enjoy the process and have some technical know-how, you'll gain a lot of satisfaction from a job well done.

You'll need to make sure the **Editing** is complete in all its stages. And when you've finished killing your **Darlings**, you'll work on the **Layout**, casting all the **Widows and Orphans** into the bitter winter night (sob).

You will need to choose the **Trim Size**, the **Fonts** and the **Illustrations**. You will need to make sure your **Cover Image** is the right size for your book, including the spine. For **eBooks**, you will need to know how to create **Flowable Text** and a clickable **Table of Contents**.

However, KDP etc want you to successfully publish your book, so there are lots of instructional videos, **Templates** and checklists to help you get it right. There are also free apps that will format your book for you, both print and eBook. (These have variable results. I don't use them, but I know people who do.)

You can also publish audiobooks on these platforms. Amazon is the biggest player,[37] distributing to Audible and iTunes as well as its own bookstore.

However, if your first, second, and third loves are writing, writing and writing, and you do not want to be bothered with the 'gubbins' of indie publishing, this might not be for you.

Cheap 📖📖📖📖

KDP charges nothing for publishing digital or print books. They even give you free **ISBN**s (expensive to buy yourself), so that's a pretty sweet deal.

Other platforms may charge for storage, updating files, ISBNs, barcodes, converting paperback to eBook etc, but even so, this is a very cost-effective way to get your books out there.

Of course, you may have to fork out for cover designers, editors, typesetters, etc., if you do not want to do these yourself, so that knocks a star off, and printing costs can explode if you want colour photos in a print book (no extra for eBooks). But for text-heavy paperbacks, this is a great option.

Profitable 📖📖📖📖📖

Because of the very low or non-existent costs, this is already a winner as far as Profitable is concerned, but when you add in the humungous royalties compared to any other route, you can understand why indie publishing is the avenue of choice for many authors.

KDP pays up to 60% royalties on paperbacks, 70% on eBooks, depending on distribution. Production costs, or transmission

---

[37] Surprise!

costs for eBooks, are deducted from your royalties and the rest goes into your bank account.

We'll use the earlier example of a £9.99 book (and you get to choose the price here). Amazon keeps 40% as their cut and in return, they list your book on Amazon internationally, store and distribute it, handle the money side of things and make a profit. You have the remaining £5.99. Printing costs, say £2.79, come off that, leaving you with £3.20 per book. A whopping 32%. That's a darned sight more than any other method.

For eBooks, you pay the transmission costs rather than printing costs, which are measured in kilobytes instead of pages. Profits are similar.

You can also order **Author Copies** of print books for the cost of printing and postage, and which you can sell for whatever price you like.

Quick

This is the fastest way to get books from hard drive to hard copy. If indie publishing were a spaceship, it would be the star ship Enterprise at warp factor 9.9

Once you have done all the preparatory work, you can upload it and go through the checks in a matter of minutes and have your book available for purchase worldwide within 48 hours.

Distribution

Amazon is the world's biggest online bookseller, by a long way. If you want your books to be in a **Bricks-and-Mortar** bookshop, you will need to use a different indie publisher such as IngramSpark instead or as well. They can list your book with wholesalers, from which bookshops buy their stock.

But for the online market, Amazon is unbeatable. Your books are listed alongside the traditionally published competition and can feature in Amazon's best-seller lists the same as any other book. Payments, currency exchange, taxes, returns, shipping and handling are all done for you, and you can sell your books anywhere in the world.

Best For ...

... authors who are keen to get their book on sale quickly, who have tech know-how and are detail-oriented for getting the minutiae right.

Best for eBooks and text-heavy paperbacks with **Greyscale** illustrations. (Colour printing ramps up the cost-per-copy enormously.)

How To

Visit Kindle Direct Publishing, Apple Books for Authors or Kobo for three of the biggest and best platforms. There is plenty of help to get you started. Remember, they want you to succeed.

Handy hint: choose the trim size first because you will need to alter the whole layout of your book if you change your mind halfway through.

I'd advise against using their in-built cover creators for the actual cover art, as these often look rather 'stock'. If you have access to a starving artist, you may be able to get a cover design for the price of a hot dinner, otherwise, if you have the pennies to pay for anything, pay for a cover. Covers sell.

Magazines and Newspapers

Hobbyist magazines are great places to write about your special interests. Make sure articles are very well researched though, because your laser-eyed readers will soon spot any mistakes.[38]

In magazines aimed at a broader audience, short stories are still a popular feature. Opinion pieces and poems, especially humorous ones, can fill an odd corner.

Local newspapers are often keen for copy. If you have interesting local knowledge, you might even end up with a regular column!

Ratings

Likely:	📖📖📖
Low Hassle:	📖📖📖📖📖
Cheap:	📖📖📖📖📖
Profitable:	📖📖📖
Quick:	📖📖📖
Distribution:	📖📖📖📖
Best for:	short stories, non-fiction articles, humorous poems.

---

[38] Rail enthusiasts will pick your bones clean if you say that the signalling code for Leeds from the Wharfedale branch was 3-1 when everyone *knows* it was 2-2-2. Honestly, plebs!

Likely 📖📖📖

As with traditional publishers, magazine publishers are looking for material that will sell. Check their website and see if they are open to **Submissions**. Make sure you choose a magazine that is a good fit for your writing style and stick rigidly to their **Submission Guidelines**.

Most well-known magazines have in-house writing teams, so it's good to set your sights a little lower than Vogue or the Times Literary Supplement, at least to start with.

On the plus side, there are literally thousands of lesser-known **Periodicals** on every subject you can imagine. So if you have a niche interest in, say, Indonesian warthog wrestling, I betcha there's a magazine out there just waiting to give window to your wisdom.

To illustrate, here are some genuine magazines: *Portable Restroom Operator*,[39] *Spudman*,[40] and the high-octane, fast-living, tell-all tabloid that is *Recumbent Cycling News*.[41]

Low Hassle 📖📖📖📖📖

Similar to **Traditional Publishing**, newspapers and magazines do all the **Editing**, **Typesetting**, illustrations etc for you, so there is no work beyond the initial composition and any re-writes that your editor thinks necessary.

---

[39] Yup, it's about Portaloos.

[40] Sadly, not about a new superhero. Although that's a book that needs writing, don't you think?

[41] Steady now.

Cheap

There should be no costs to the author. Beware of publications that charge a 'reading fee' when you submit your article. This might be a scam to make money from hopeful authors.

Profitable

Not a bad way to make money from your writing. If an article does not sell, you've only lost a few hundred words, a couple of thousand at most. Compare that to a book, which might be ten times as long and take ten times longer to produce.

Some periodicals pay a flat fee (perhaps £20 - £50 per article), some pay by the word (5p – 20p per word), while others do not pay at all, your reward being exposure.[42]

It's up to you whether the prestige of being published is enough for you, or if you want the mucky moolah in your mitt.

Quick

This very much depends on how often the magazine or newspaper is published. Newspapers tend to have a very short turnaround, so be sure to keep to **Deadlines**, or feel the editor's wrath!

Magazines are less frantic, but even annual issues will be speedier than traditional publishing. But bear in mind that magazines may be working six months in advance, so don't expect to see your work on the supermarket shelves next week.

---

[42] Seeing your name in print, I mean, not having a double-page spread in *Grubby Raincoat Weekly* ... oh, never mind.

Distribution

Specialist magazines cater for small but dedicated audiences. In younger days I remember eagerly devouring every month's Gauge '0' Guild[43] magazine.

So while distribution might be lower in numbers, you get a deep rather than a broad spread, reaching many interested readers.

Best For ...

... specialist non-fiction articles and short fiction. Magazines are often the best places to get poetry published. (Many traditional publishers have a blanket 'No' for poems.)

How To

The organisation *Authors Publish* have a useful newsletter listing publishers who are accepting **Submissions**. Most are for books, but the listing regularly features magazines seeking submissions in various **Genres**.

The Writers and Artists' Yearbook is an invaluable source of information for this method of publishing. You can find it in your local library or online.

---

[43] For those of you who have read that out loud, I can assure you that it is a venerable publication for aficionados of model railways twice the size 'double-O', and nothing to do with a rather jolly chap named Joseph.

Academic Press

Here we tiptoe up the stairs of the ivory tower and peep behind the velvet curtains of academia. There are myriad worthy tomes published by **University Presses** which keep the shelves of their libraries from floating away, and there are academic **Journals** with such thrilling names as the *Journal of Negative Results in BioMedicine* or the *IEEE Transactions on Advanced Packaging* (oh, whoop) as well as more famous ones such as *The Lancet* and *Nature*.

But while these might not feature on most people's Christmas lists, academic journals are important for finding out *stuff*. Here, the worthies of the world distribute discoveries and expound inventions. Without them, the world would be a duller place, and we'd not have cool things like lasers and microwave ovens.[44]

Ratings

Likely: 📖📖📖📖
Low Hassle: 📖📖
Cheap: 📖📖📖📖📖
Profitable: 📖
Quick: 📖📖
Distribution: 📖📖📖
Best for: Significant non-fiction

---

[44] My esteemed editor points out that lasers and microwave ovens are hot, not cool. I counter that, as parts of the electromagnetic spectrum other than infra-red, they are not of themselves hot, but forms of energy that can heat. So there. Thwwwwpt!

Likely 📖📖📖📖

If you can write something for an academic journal, you are fairly likely to be published, simply because there are not that many people submitting papers.[45]

As well as the usual editorial standards, papers have to pass **Peer-Review** before publication, that is, they are checked over by experts in the field. So if yours passes muster, that is a very large pat on the back for you.

Low Hassle 📖📖

Nope. Aside from being able to write coherently, you need original research to at least master's level. And then there's the **Academic Referencing**. Oh, the agony.

That said, if you clear those hurdles, the rest is a doddle. You've probably written up your thesis anyway, so you'll only need to re-write for the new audience (making sure you stick to the **House Style**), chuck out the literature review, cut the rest by about half, and Robert is your mother's brother.

Cheap 📖📖📖📖📖

Should cost you nothing.

Journals generally make their money by selling (expensive) subscriptions to libraries and universities. Some journals are free to read and charge the university that hosts the research instead, but you should pay nothing either way.

---

[45] Articles become papers at this level. No idea why.

Profitable 📖

The flip side is that you get paid nothing as well. You submit work to an academic journal so that you can say you are a published mathematician or a published theologian.[46] Some university posts require you to publish regularly, but if you're one of those people you'll know all about that by now.

Quick 📖📖

Beyond the usual turnaround time for editing and production, your paper has to be reviewed by suitable academics. They often ask for re-writes and this adds considerably to the already lengthy process, so don't expect to see your work in print this side of 6 months. Longer if it's an annual publication.

Distribution 📖📖📖

Like niche magazines, academic journals have a deep rather than broad appeal. You won't find them in bookshops, nor most public libraries. Instead, they'll be in the departmental libraries of universities and on the bookshelves of the movers and shakers in your world.

Submitting your work to academic journals is more about increasing the general level of cleverness in the world than gaining international fame and a guest appearance on Celebrity Come Dine with Me.[47]

But 'Academic Publications' is a nice subheading for your CV.

---

[46] Or both, if you believe that $e^{i\pi} + 1 = 0$ proves that God is a mathematician.

[47] A considerable blessing, if you ask me.

Best For...

... that PhD thesis you have been using to prop up a wobbly table leg. Dust it off and see if you can condense it to 6,000 words.

How To

Taylor and Francis is a good place to start. They are the umbrella publishers of a huge range of academic journals in both arts and sciences. Scan through the shelves of your departmental library to find suitable titles.

Submissions Guidelines are specific to each journal and, as I may have mentioned before, you should abide by them as closely as if they were handed down on tablets of stone.[48]

---

[48] Rather more closely, if you take a look at Exodus 32!

Blogging

A **Blog** is a great way to get your work out there and can serve as a way into other methods such as **Traditional** and **Indie Publishing**.

Blogging is perfect for refining your **Target Audience**, for building a readership and for publicising your new book to people who already like what you write.

You will need to post regularly to build an audience, but posts are short, usually 100-1,000 words. I put two posts a week on my blog and forward them automatically to social media and my **Mailing List**. This gives me a reach of several thousand readers twice a week, and some of my books are collections of popular blog posts.

Ratings

Likely:	📖📖📖📖📖
Low Hassle:	📖📖📖📖
Cheap:	📖📖📖📖
Profitable:	📖
Quick:	📖📖📖📖📖
Distribution:	📖📖
Best for:	Short articles about whatever gets you buzzing.

Likely

One of the joys of blogging is that anyone can publish anything.

One of the pains is that anyone can publish *anything*. And they do.

The blogosphere is awash with pearls of perfect prose, witty wisdom and succulent sentences, all tangled in the seaweed of a million cat videos, life hacks that don't work and someone's Uncle Arthur's bunion op.

Low Hassle

If you want to generate a following, you need to publish regularly. That means producing content at least every week.

You might regard this as a bad thing if that's a hassle. On the other hand, it's a good discipline for writing, and after a year you will have a lot of material built up. Instant book!

Depending on your technical skills, you may need some help in getting a web address (**Domain Name**) and setting up the site hosting and mailing list, but once it's all in place, it's pretty simple to add posts.

Cheap

You can get a basic blog site for free from lots of providers, but they usually include the blog provider's name, such as froggyblog1234.blogosphere.com.

If you want to look more professional, it's good to have your own web address. You'll pay a small fee per year to buy a domain name such as froggyblog.co.uk, and a similar amount for web hosting (storing your website and handling emails).

Actually posting a blog and maintaining a mailing list usually costs nothing. Once you get over a certain number of daily hits or size of mailing list, hosting sites might start charging you the business package, but by that time you'll be looking for a holiday home in the Bahamas, so it shouldn't worry you.

Profitable 📖

Blogging itself does not earn you anything. You are gaining readers, a mailing list and practice in your writing skills.

Some bloggers earn money by affiliate links, advertising or sponsorship, but that's a whole different kettle of fish, and I don't like fish-flavoured tea.[49]

Quick 📖📖📖📖📖

Instant. You write a blog post and press 'Publish'.

Job done. Cup of ~~sardine~~ tea.

Distribution 📖📖

This depends enormously on your readership. Some blogs get a thousand hits every day while others reach a dozen a year, and eight of those are the author's friends.[50]

It's up to you to find your readers, and there's no sure-fire method. Finding someone with a similar blog and swapping posts can help, as well as posting on social media such as

---

[49] A fish kettle is a large cooking pot, not a kettle that you'd use to make tea. But the joke still works, I think.

[50] The other four hits are the author checking if it looks alright.

Facebook and Instagram. Posting regularly helps a lot, but not too often or it comes across as spam.

Bottom line: It may take several years of posting content to gain a decent group of readers. But that's great practice for you.

Best For …

… building an audience and testing out material.

Write about what makes you tick. Write about the characters in your book. Write about your day. *Don't* write about your Uncle Arthur's bunion op.

How To

You can use one of the blog-off-the-shelf sites but, to be honest, it'll show. That's fine if it's a hobbyist site and you don't expect much traffic. But if you want to look more professional, get your own domain name and install blogging software such as WordPress.

Social Publishing

A popular publishing medium with Generation Internet is the social-media style website. These are places where members can post their writing and read what others have written.

Most sites have no editorial oversight, so anyone can post. Most are free, so anyone can read. And most are huge, so there's a **Niche** for your writing, no matter what **Genre**.

The quality of writing is variable, naturally, but the good seems to rise to the top and you can find some excellent fiction series. A notable success(ful) story is Anna Todd's *After*, which started as serialised fiction on Wattpad, became a best-selling book series and ended up on Netflix. It's also how Charles Dickens started,[51] if he's more your cup of tea.

Social publishing is a good way to hone your craft and increase in confidence as a writer. Readers can rate your stories, and this gives you useful feedback.

Ratings

Likely: 📖📖📖📖📖
Low Hassle: 📖📖📖📖📖
Cheap: 📖📖📖📖📖
Profitable: 📖
Quick: 📖📖📖📖📖
Distribution: 📖📖📖📖
Best for: chapter-at-a-time fan stories, poetry.

---

[51] Not on Wattpad and Netflix, obviously. I meant as serialised fiction.

Likely 📖📖📖📖📖

Posting your prose to a writing website is as easy as the ratio of circumference to diameter.[52]

You do not have to align with a magazine's themed issue. You do not have to convince an editor that your story is saleable. You do not need your paper peer-reviewed by egg-heads. Simply sign up to your preferred site and post.

You are 100% likely to be able to post your writing. And therein lies both the strength and weakness of this route.

Low Hassle 📖📖📖📖📖

Very low hassle, particularly if you are Gen-Z, born with a smartphone welded to your fingertips.

Cheap 📖📖📖📖📖

Free. What more is there to say?

Most of the sites are funded by annoying ads that pop up while you are reading, or by subscriptions that make the annoying ads go away.

Profitable 📖

Generally none, but some sites, such as Wattpad, will pay popular writers. This route is more for those wanting a paying hobby than earning a living, but you can still say you've been paid for your writing, which is a feather in anyone's cap.

---

[52] Pi. Bit of geeky humour. Sorry. I'll crawl back under my rock now.

Quick 📖📖📖📖📖

How quickly can you hit 'Send'?

Distribution 📖📖📖📖

Available anywhere the internet can reach, so unless your **Target Audience** is in the middle of The Great Sandy Desert,[53] you're sorted.

Wattpad, for example, has around 90 million readers, so someone, somewhere, is bound to like your work whether that be the ever-popular **Fan-fic** and fantasy genres, or the more niche Croatian romantic murder mystery cook book.

However, the very popularity of these sites can mean that your writing gets lost amongst all the others. You can use tags to help readers to find your work, and some places will highlight similar items ('If you liked that, what not try ...'), but it's still pretty hard to stand out from the madding crowd.

Best For ...

... fan-fiction writers, authors wanting to try their hand at a new style / genre without committing to a whole book at once, poets, and just-have-a-go writers.

Authors and readers on these sites tend to be the net-savvy among us, so readership is strongly correlated with age. If you are writing a review of retirement homes, this method is probably not your best bet. If you are writing an alternative storyline to the *Harry Potter* universe or lyrics for the next *Hamilton*, fill your boots!

---

[53] Don't you just love Aussie naming conventions?

How To

Two of the biggest[54] writing sites are *AO3* (Archive Of Our Own) and *Wattpad*. According to my teenaged daughter, who spends hours each day reading on these sites (I'm not complaining), *Wattpad* has a greater proportion of kid-written fiction, whereas *AO3* writers are mainly adults.

Both platforms mainly host serialised fiction which is a great way to keep readers returning regularly for 'the next thrilling instalment!' Poets have *AllPoetry* and *Poetry Foundation*.

Publishing is very simple. You create an account and upload your text file. Be sure to use plenty of tags so that readers can find your work.

Radish Fiction is a moderated site, with corresponding higher quality content and they pay **Royalties** (be still, my beating heart) funded by reader subscriptions. You submit **Proposals** as you would to a **Traditional Publisher**, with the usual reference to **Submission Guidelines**.

Kindle Vella is the new broom in this cupboard, and promises to sweep a more professional route to serial book publishing. It works similarly to their **KDP** platform and benefits from Amazon's huge reach in the **eBook** market.

Many authors engage in **Freeconomics**, publishing the first few chapters for free to get readers into the story who will then (hopefully) pay for the rest of the book.

---

[54] At the time of writing, these things change quickly.

Competitions

Some literary magazines and writers' societies run regular competitions with the winners' entries published as part of the prize. Educational bodies and organisations such as the BBC also run writing competitions from time to time, although these are usually aimed at children.

Rather like winning Great British Bake Off or X-Factor, coming top in a prestigious writing competition can be the springboard to international fame and fortune. Or not.

But whether the lofty peaks of celebrity await or the gently rolling foothills of a nice post on Facebook, winning a competition gives you great publicity and a valuable top line for your writer's CV. It also gives you credibility and validation – two things that most writers crave as a dragon craves gold.

Ratings

Likely: 📖📖
Low Hassle: 📖📖📖📖
Cheap: 📖📖📖📖
Profitable: 📖📖
Quick: 📖📖📖
Distribution: 📖📖
Best for: short fiction, non-fiction and poetry, often on a given theme.

Likely 📖📖

Competitions have fewer winners than entrants, so this is not a guaranteed route to seeing your words in print, but it's worth a shot. Even if you don't win, you can send your writing to a magazine or online writing site, so nothing's wasted.

Low Hassle 📖📖📖📖

Competitions tend to be for shorter pieces – essays and poems usually – so it's not a huge time commitment. The tricky bit is writing a prize-worthy piece, but assuming you've done that, you're set.

Cheap 📖📖📖📖

Generally, competitions are free to enter. Some may have a small entry fee to cover the costs of judging and prizes, which is fair enough.

Beware of competitions with larger fees, though. They may be scams aimed at making money from aspiring authors.

Profitable 📖📖

The magazine or literary society may offer a monetary prize. On the other hand, they may feel that the kudos of winning and being published are sufficient rewards.

Probably not a way to make your living, but how nice to buy something with money that you have earned by writing!

Quick 📖📖📖

The speed of publication for competitions in a magazine is the same as for a regular edition, six months give or take. Literary societies open **Submissions** a few weeks before the prize-giving, so that's shorter, but they're usually only once a year so you'll have to wait.

Distribution

Distribution for magazine competitions is the same as for magazines in general, with the added highlight of your name being on the cover as a competition winner. The internet means you can enter competitions internationally as well (assuming you write the correct language).

For literary societies, the announcing of the winner will probably be the main feature of an exhibition, so that's great publicity if slightly preaching to the converted.

Best For ...

... short fiction, themed essays and poetry. These are the most popular formats for competitions although others exist. Understandably, judges do not want to wade through 500 entries each of 100,000 words, so if you are looking to publish a three-volume novel, you'll probably need a different route.

How To

Join a local or online writers' society (good to do anyway) and keep your ears open for upcoming events. Check notice boards in libraries and of course, there's always t'interweb.

Part C

Glossary

This glossary has grown a lot bigger than I expected. **Beta Readers** kept suggesting things, and every time I wrote about a word, I found I needed a new entry!

I hope you find it useful, helping to demystify all the jargon and mystic runes with which publishing abounds.

Words in **bold** are listed in the glossary.

A

About the Author
A page of an author's **Website**, or part of the **Back Matter** of a book, which introduces the author along with a photo. Often less formal than a **Bio**, this is the place to engage your readers with fun facts about your pets.

Abstract
A summary of an academic article that is printed before the main text. In contrast to a book **Blurb**, an abstract gives away the ending.

Academic Referencing
Strictly formatted **Footnotes** or inline tags directing the reader to the source of a quotation or idea. Used in papers submitted to academic **Journals** and some other non-fiction writing. References may be expanded in a **Bibliography** at the end.

Acknowledgements
Part of the **Front** or **Back Matter**. The author thanks those who have helped, often role models, family members or staff.

Acquisitions Editor
The person at a **Traditional Publisher** who first sees submitted **Manuscripts** (and issues the **Rejections Slips**).

Advance
An advance payment of **Royalties** from a traditional publisher. You will only be offered this if the publisher is certain that they will sell enough books to cover your advance, so it's more for the likes of Tim Peake than plebs like you and me.

Note that this isn't free money. It comes off your royalties later.

Advance(d) Copies
Free copies of your book sent to relevant authors, magazines, and social media influencers before the **Publication Date** in the hope that they will review it, provide **Endorsements** for your **Blurb**, or invite you for an interview.

Agent
A literary agent is an intermediary between author and publisher. They submit book **Proposals** to appropriate editors, negotiate **Contracts** and ensure **Royalties** are paid promptly. Typically an agent has many contacts in the publishing industry and deep knowledge of what sells.

You do not have to have an agent, but some publishers will only accept **Submissions** from agents, not from authors.

Reputable agents do not charge a reading fee, nor any fee for submitting your work to publishers. They make their money as a cut of your royalties (which means they want the best deal for you), so if one tries to charge you up front, walk away.

Alignment
Chaotic Good, Lawful Neutral or … No, sorry, that's Dungeons and Dragons.

In publishing, alignment is the arrangement of text within a column. Left-aligned text is neat on the left and ragged on the right, while right-aligned text is the opposite. **Justified** text is neat at both edges. This paragraph is justified.

Images can also have an alignment, often with text flowing around them. Images in **eBooks** must have no alignment. That is, they must be 'in-line' with the **Flowable Text**.

Appendices
Part of the **Back Matter**, appearing immediately after the main text. Appendices contain additional reference material such as maps or datasets. If more than one, they are Appendix A, Appendix B, etc.

Ascender
The part of a letter that reaches above the top of a letter o, such as the stalk of the letter d. Opposite of a **Descender**.

Aspect Ratio
The width to height ratio of an image, page or screen, such as 16:9 for computer monitors. Tall images are **Portrait**. Wider images are **Landscape**.

Audiobook
A sound recording of the full or abridged text of a book that can be purchased online or borrowed from a library (usually as a CD) in the same way as a paper book.

Author Copies
In **Traditional Publishing**, complimentary copies of a book given to the author on publication. In **Indie Publishing**, copies of the book that the author buys at cost, should they wish. In **Hybrid Publishing**, the discounted copies that the author agrees to buy.

Author Services
Stand-alone businesses providing parts of the publication process as a service to self-publishing authors. These include illustrators and cover designers, editors of various types, **eBook** converters, and print-on-demand (**POD**) platforms.

B

Backlist

Also called the back catalogue. The list of an author's or publisher's previous books that are still for sale. They are not being actively promoted, but they are not **Out of Print**.

Back Matter

Optional pages after the main text. These pages often have no numbers and where present are in this order:

- **Acknowledgements** (if not in the Front Matter)
- **Appendices**
- **Endnotes**
- **Glossary**
- **Bibliography**, **References** or **Further Reading**
- **Index**
- **About the Author**
- **Other Publications**

Barcode

The pattern of thin and thick lines on the back of a book that encodes its **ISBN** and optionally its **RRP**. Some **Self-Publishing** platforms charge a mint for generating a barcode from your ISBN, but you can get a conversion more cheaply or for free elsewhere. Make sure it is a high-**Resolution** image, though.

Beta Readers

When you have completed your **First Draft**, given it a thorough edit, cut out bits that don't work, swapped a few sections around, added a new ending and edited again, it might be time for you to peep out from your cocoon and find out how your writing looks to other people. These people are your beta readers.

These are not professional editors; instead, they are might be friends and family, or people from your writing group.[55] The idea is to gather opinions from real people who might actually read your book. Choose people who will be honest (but kind).

Bibliography

A list of relevant books that have been used in the preparation of the manuscript. Different from **Further Reading**, a list of books that might interest the reader, and from **References**, which are the works cited or alluded to in the text. You would usually only have one of these three.

Big Five/Four (The)

Publishing houses that are responsible for the vast majority of print books in circulation. Originally five, Penguin acquired Simon & Schuster leaving Penguin Random House, Macmillan, Hachette, and HarperCollins. They are home to many famous **Imprints** such as Dorling Kindersley, Fontana and Doubleday.

Binding

Joining pages into a book, usually with thread or glue to form a spine. Binding types include perfect (most paperbacks), spiral-bound and case-bound. Some open flat, others don't.

Bio

A short introduction, often noting your credentials in the topic. It can be found at the top or bottom of an article, or in a List of Contributors at the back of a multi-author book. More formal than **About the Author**, your bio may be limited to a couple of lines or might be a couple of paragraphs on the flap of a **Dust Jacket**.

---

[55] You *are* part of a writing group, aren't you?

Bleed

Extending an image beyond the normal printing area, such as off the edge of the page or across the **Gutter**. This technique is used for cover images and for children's picture books or cookery books. Bleed images extend into regions that will be trimmed, so there should be no text or crucial parts of an image in these areas.

Block Quote

A longer quotation set as an indented block within the main text, usually without quotation marks. Rules for block quotes may be given in a **Style Guide**.

Not the same as a **Pull Quote**, which duplicates a small section of the text as a stylistic feature.

Blog

Short for we**b log**. This is a regularly updated online journal on a particular subject, often with an associated **Mailing List**.

Many writers find blogging a useful tool for finding out what their readers like, for producing material that later becomes a book, or for connecting with their readers. It is useful to have your own **Domain Name**, such as fayrowland.co.uk, as this improves **Branding**.

Blog Tour

Making guest appearances on other authors' blogs to promote your new book. Can be part of a **Virtual Book Tour**.

Blue Pencil

Traditionally used in **Copy Editing** to make corrections to a **Hard Copy**. The term is used figuratively to mean deciding which pieces of a manuscript need to be altered or removed.

Blurb

The promotional material on the back cover of a book or the description on an online bookshop. Can include **Endorsements** from reviewers who have received an **Advanced Copy**.

Your blurb will introduce your main character and their quest but will not reveal the ending, unlike a **Synopsis** for a book **Proposal** or an **Abstract**.

Book Tour

An author's promotional tour around libraries, bookshops and broadcasters, usually immediately after **Publication Date**. Events might include readings, book signings and interviews. Also available online as **Virtual Book Tour**.

Branding

Branding shows readers what to expect and encourages new readers to try your books. Agatha Christie, for example, is a brand of cosy murder mysteries.

You can improve your branding by being active on social media, having a **Website** or regularly posting to a **Blog** so that readers come to know your name.

You can improve book branding by following conventions in your **Genre** such as trim size and word count and help readers to find books in a series by keeping the **Cover Images** similar and giving them related titles.

Bricks-and-Mortar

Actual, physical bookshops stocking actual, physical books.

By-line

The name, and sometimes photograph, of the author at the head or foot of an article in a magazine or newspaper.

C

Camera-Ready

An image or page that has passed **Proof Reading** and is ready to be printed. The term comes from offset printing, where the final layout was photographed, and a printing plate made from the negative. In modern **DTP**, it simply means finished.

Caption

A description or title underneath an image.

CMYK (Cyan, Magenta, Yellow, Key)

A way of describing colours by the amounts of the secondary colours (cyan, magenta and yellow), in decimal numbers out of 100. Key is black.

CMYK is used in domestic inkjet printers and in commercial four-colour printing where Ikea Yellow is 2, 11, 96, 0.

At school, you may have been taught that blue, red and yellow were the primary colours. That is a mangled version of cyan (blueish), magenta (reddish) and yellow.[56]

Co-Authoring

Writing a book with other authors, all of whom are named.

If one party is a celebrity with limited writing skills, the writer's contribution is to render the celebrity's words in a palatable form, while the celebrity contributes their fame and salacious gossip. This is often seen as more ethical than **Ghostwriting** where the actual writer is invisible.

---

[56] Which explains why you could never get black by mixing those three colours of paint. You can with cyan, magenta and yellow.

Column Inch / SCC (Single Column Centimetre)
The area of a newspaper equal to one column wide by one inch or one cm deep. Used to pay authors who write columns.

Column Rule
Vertical **Hairline** used to separate columns of type in a newspaper or multi-column book.

Commercial Printers
A company that produces your book to order. They may offer services such as **Layout** or basic **Copy Editing**, but they make their money from printing; they do not distribute books. These are reputable companies, unlike **Vanity Presses**.

Commissioned
A **Manuscript** that you have been asked to write as opposed to **Speculative** submissions. Commissioned pieces are almost certain to be published. Let's face it, if the editor likes you enough to ask, you'd have to do something pretty spectacular to mess it up.

Content Editing
The first major stage of editing, also called structural editing or developmental editing. This looks at the big picture: the **Story Arc**, character development and, for non-fiction, organisation and logical progression.

Contents
In print books, the contents page lists the sections or chapters and their page numbers.

In **eBooks**, the table of contents (**TOC**) uses hyperlinks instead of page numbers to help readers navigate the text. The TOC is mandatory for eBooks.

Contract

A legally binding agreement between a publisher and an author. It stipulates such matters as **Deadlines**, **Royalties**, **Author Copies** and publishing **Rights**. Literary **Agents** can obtain the best contract for you and advise on details.

Co-Publishing

Also called hybrid publishing, this is a halfway house between traditional book deals and author-funded publishing. The author agrees to purchase a portion of the **Print Run** as their contribution to the costs, and the publishing company funds and distributes the rest.

Beware of potential **Vanity Presses** who will push the majority of the financial burden onto the author. Check your contract and be sure that the price and quantity of **Author Copies** are commensurate with what you think you will be able to sell.

Copy

Not the stuff that comes out of a photocopier. In publishing terms, copy means the written material. Copy is edited by a (guess what) **Copy Editor** and typeset to produce proofs. A **Proof Reader** gives these a final check before printing.

Copy Editing

Looking for **SPaG** errors, checking for variations in tense or **Voice**, and making sure headings, lists, **References** etc. are consistent and in line with any **Style Guide**.

In non-fiction and historical fiction **Genres**, a copy editor may also check facts. Specialist non-fiction, such as textbooks, require specialist copy editors.

Copy editors often perform the job of a line editor too, but when the two are separate, a line editor is more focussed on the writing style and use of language, making sure that the language flows well and has the right **Tone**.

Line editing comes before copy editing, and both come before **Proof Reading**.

Copyright

The (complex) laws surrounding ownership of intellectual property. Ask someone who knows more than me.

Your **Agent**, should you have one, can advise or you can search for 'intellectual property' on your government's website.

Copyright Page

The page at the start of a book that contains the copyright notice, publisher etc. It comes directly after the title page and before any other items in the **Front Matter**.

Cover Image

The artwork and text of your book's cover, and the only part of your book that most people will ever see. Sadly, books are judged almost exclusively by their covers, so put a lot of care into this. Make sure your cover looks good when small, since it will appear as a **Thumbnail** in online bookshops.

In **Traditional Publishing**, the cover design is managed for you. If you are **Indie Publishing**, you will need to provide a **Camera-Ready** cover image that is the right size for your book including the spine. This is an area where professional **Author Services** can help.

D

Darlings

Your darlings are the parts of your manuscript that you love and are reluctant to lose, even when they spoil the work as a whole. They are the reason it is so hard to edit your own work.

> *"Kill your darlings, kill your darlings, even when it breaks your egocentric little scribbler's heart, kill your darlings."*
> — Stephen King

Deadline

The date by which you must give your **Manuscript** to your publisher – or die![57]

Dedication

Part of a book's **Front Matter**, usually on the **Recto** page immediately after the **Copyright Page**. Here are some of my favourite dedications:

- To my creditors, who remain a permanent source of inspiration.
  — Michael Moorcock, *The Steel Tsar*,
- For Colin Firth. You're a really great guy, but I'm married, so I think we should just be friends.
  — Shannon Hale, *Austenland*
- To my wife Marganit and my children Ella Rose and Daniel Adam without whom this book would have been completed two years earlier.
  — Joseph J. Rotman, *Algebraic Topology*

---

[57] Slight exaggeration. But only slight.

Descender
The part of a letter that dips below the baseline, such as the tail of a y. Opposite of an **Ascender**.

Developmental Editing
See **Content Editing**.

Disclaimer
A statement, usually at the front of a book or at the top of an **Op-Ed**, that distances the publisher or writer from the views expressed within: by an interviewee, for example.

Display Font / Typeface
A decorative **Typeface** used for headings and titles, usually 18 points or larger. Some typefaces might be illegible in smaller **Point Sizes** or unreadable in large quantities. Use sparingly!

Domain Name / URL (Uniform Resource Locator)
A domain is a registered address on the World Wide Web that identifies your resources, commonly a **Website** and email address. A URL points to a specific page on your website.

You can purchase a name from one of the many domain name servers, usually on a yearly basis. You will also need a host to store your website and forward your emails.

Drop(ped) Cap(ital)
A typographical feature in which the first letter of a chapter is rendered in a larger **Point Size**, and possibly a **Display Font**.

A RELATED EFFECT is enlarging or capitalising the first words of a chapter.

DPI (Dots per Inch)

A measure of **Resolution** for images and printers. The number of **Pixels** in one linear inch.

An image measuring 3" by 4" at 300dpi is 900px wide by 1,200px high. The image would contain 1,080,000px in total (900 x 1,200), or just over 1 megapixel.

DRM (Digital Rights Management)

Software included with some **eBooks** to stop them from being illegally shared, copied or stored.

DTP (Desk-Top Publishing)

Page **Layout** software, such as PageMaker, that converts words and images into **Print-Ready** pages.

Much as it tries to be, Microsoft Word is not a DTP program.

Dust Jacket / Dust Cover

A full-colour printed paper cover that folds around a (usually plainer) hardback book, tucking inside the boards. Additional information, such as an author **Bio**, can be printed on the folded-in sections.

E

eBook

An electronic version of a paper book, which can be stored and read on an **eReader**, phone or computer. Two major file types are **ePub** and **Mobi**.

Editing

The stages between **First Draft** and publication.

Different pieces of writing will have different journeys through the editorial process, and some stages may need repeating or might be merged.

The major stages are **Structural** (aka content / developmental) editing, which looks at the overall flow of the piece, then **Line** and **Copy Editing** which examine the language style and the nitty-gritty of spelling, punctuation and grammar.

When all is correct, the final stage is **Proof Reading**, which catches anything that escaped the earlier nets, and errors introduced during **Typesetting**.

Elevator Pitch

Also called a hook. A one-breath summary of your book.[58]

The various book summaries, from shortest to longest:
Tagline / Strapline - snappy catchphrase
Logline - one-ish sentence
Elevator pitch – a few sentences
Synopsis - one page (including spoilers!)

---

[58] The idea is that you can corner a prospective publisher in a lift and get your message across between floors. Or you can say, "Halt turbo lift!" like they do in Star Trek whenever they want to discuss something.

Here are examples for *Lord of the Rings*.

Strapline: *One Ring to Rule them All.*

Logline: *A daring hobbit and his band of mismatched adventurers must destroy a powerful ring before it destroys them.*

Elevator Pitch: *Short, jovial and chubby, Frodo is an unlikely adventurer, but his journey with fellow Hobbits, Elves and a grumpy Dwarf ends in a battle for The One Ring. Aided by a wizard and the mysterious Aragorn, who will finally rule Middle Earth?*

The synopsis is longer and goes into more detail, including the ending.

Embedded Fonts

Information about the fonts used in a document that is retained within the document itself. This ensures that a **PDF**, for example, prints correctly when unusual **Display Fonts** are used. Most **POD** platforms require embedded fonts.

Em Dash

A short horizontal line, the width of a letter m. Longer than an **En Dash** and often surrounded by spaces. Used for setting off a parenthetical aside – such as this – from the rest of a sentence.

Not to be confused with an underscore which sits at the baseline of the text.

En Dash

A short horizontal line, the width of a letter n. Shorter than an **Em Dash** and often conflated with the **Hyphen** because most word processors only have two lengths of dash.

End Matter
See **Back Matter.**

Endorsement
A recommendation by an influential person or reviewer, often used as part of the **Blurb**. One of the main reasons to send out **Advanced Copies** is to garner endorsements.

Endnote
A superscript number or symbol in the main text directing the reader to additional material at the end of the chapter or book. **Footnotes** are similar but are grouped at the bottom of the page.

Enlargement
A picture that has been made bigger than its original. This lowers the **Resolution** of the image and can result in poor quality. Usually, 300**dpi** is the minimum resolution for printing.

ePub
A widely-supported file format for **eBooks**, used for iPads, Nook and many other **eReaders**. Other formats include **PDF** and **Mobi**.

eReader
A portable device similar to a tablet that downloads, stores and displays **eBooks**. Kindle is Amazon's eReader. Laptops and phones can act as eReaders by downloading appropriate apps.

F

Fan-fic(tion)
A popular sub-genre where fans of popular fictional universes extend stories with character variations and new adventures.

Occasionally, fan-fic becomes best-selling books, such as P.D. James' *Death Comes to Pemberley* or *Moriarty* by Anthony Horowitz, but more usually this is Gen-Z on social publishing websites.

First Draft
The first (very) rough version of your piece, before revision or **Structural Editing**. Don't show your first draft to anyone who doesn't love you.

Flash Fiction
A sub-genre characterised by being very short: usually below 3000 words and sometimes fewer than 100.

A classic flash tragedy is 'For Sale: Baby Shoes, Never Worn'.

Flowable Text
Text that is not bound to a position on a page so that if the user enlarges the text, the last words flow to the next page. Flowable text will also reformat for **Portrait** or **Landscape** devices. Most **eBooks** have flowable text.

Having no set page numbers, flowable text is navigated via hyperlinks in a clickable table of contents (**TOC**).

Font
The specific combination of **Typeface**, **Point Size** and **Variant**. Eg Calibri, 12pt, Roman.

Foreword
An introduction to a book by a respected authority in the field.

Footer
Text at the bottom of every page, usually on the outer corners, commonly containing page numbers.

Footnote
A superscript number or symbol directing the reader to additional material at the bottom of the page. **Endnotes** are similar but are grouped at the end of the chapter or book.

Freeconomics
Giving away the first few chapters of a book, or the first book in a series, in order to sell the others. A popular strategy in the **eBook** market where there are no postage costs.

Front Matter
Optional pages before the main text, either unnumbered or with Roman numerals. Where present they are in this order:

- **Title Page**
- **Copyright Page**
- **Dedication**
- **Contents**
- **Foreword**
- **Preface**
- **Acknowledgements**
- **Introduction**

Further Reading
A list of books that the reader might like to consult. Different from a **Bibliography** (works that have been read or referred to) and from **References** (works cited).

G

Genre
The categories of books that you might find on library shelves. Examples of fiction genres include sci-fi, teen romance, fantasy and crime fiction, while non-fiction genres include instruction manuals, biographies, cookery books and true crime.

Ghostwriting
Writing a book for someone else (often a celebrity) without being acknowledged or credited as an author. This can be considered deceptive. Ghostwriting is usually **Work-for-Hire**, with the celebrity receiving the **Royalties**. This differs from **Co-Authoring**, in which the writer is credited.

Glossary
This.

Greyscale / Grayscale
Images made of black, white and shades of grey as opposed to full-colour images.

Greyscale images are considerably cheaper to print than colour because they only require a single impression in black ink instead of four carefully aligned prints for the four-colour separation process (**CMYK**).

Gutter
The middle margin of a book or magazine, usually wider than the outer margins to allow for **Binding**. You may notice that this page has a larger margin on the inside. That is the gutter.

H

Hairline
A thin line between the main text and **Footnotes**, for example.

Half Tone
A way of producing images using varying-sized dots. Large dots make a darker tone and smaller dots, lighter. This produces **Greyscale** images with black ink, or full-colour images using four half-tone images in the colour separations (**CMYK**).

Hard Copy
A paper version of your **Manuscript**. Most publishers do not accept hard copy **Submissions**.

Header
Information at the top of every page in the main text of a book, commonly book title, chapter, author or page number.

Hook
See **Elevator Pitch**.

House Style
The internal **Style Guide** for a publishing house or publication.

Hybrid Publishing
See **Co-publishing**.

Hyphen
The shortest of all the dashes, used for compound words,[59] splitting words at line breaks and for number ranges.

---

[59] Such as un-hyphenated, ironically.

I

Imprint

A subdivision of a large publishing house, particularly one of **The Big Five/Four**, often with a specialist interest. Virago Press is a feminist imprint of Hachette, and Zondervan is a Christian imprint of HarperCollins.

Index

A list of important words and the pages on which they occur. Part of the **Back Matter**, coming after the **Bibliography**.

Indie Publishing

Short for independent, indie publishing uses the power of modern Print-on-Demand (**POD**) services to bypass **Traditional Publishers**.

Indie publishing offers high royalties and full control along with access to global markets. Some platforms will get your books into **Bricks-and-Mortar** stores.

Kindle Direct Publishing (**KDP**) is the largest platform for indie books, both **eBook** and paperback, accounting for over 80% of all indie books in the US.

Introduction

Part of the **Front Matter** along with **Foreword** and **Preface**. You will not usually need all of these.

An introduction comes immediately before chapter 1 and is written from the perspective of the text. For fiction, it may introduce background material such as how the characters arrived at the place where we meet them (literally or metaphorically). For non-fiction, it might include 'how to use this book'.

ISBN (International Standard Book Number)

A 10- or 13-digit number that uniquely identifies a book, usually represented by a barcode on the back cover.

Booksellers use ISBNs for stock management, so each version of a book, such as paperback, hardback, illustrated edition, major revision or translation, requires a different ISBN. Books that you distribute yourself, and which will not pass through a bookshop, do not need ISBNs.

Magazines, academic journals, and other periodicals do not have ISBNs. Instead, they have 8-digit ISSNs (International Standard Serial Numbers).

ISBNs are optional for **eBooks**. Neither Amazon, Barnes & Noble, Kobo nor Apple require them. However, if you use one, it must be different from the paperback version.

Traditional Publishers will assign ISBNs to the books they publish. **Indie Publishing** authors can buy ISBNs from some **Self-Publishing** platforms, or they may be provided free of charge, for example, by **KDP**.

Authors can also buy ISBNs directly from their country's distributor: Nielsen in the UK or Bowker in the US.

J

Journal (Academic)

The gold standard for scholarly, if not always easily-digestible, writing, academic journals are where the sum of human knowledge is displayed and admired. Articles describing original research are **Peer-Reviewed** and become fodder for future researchers' and students' **References**.

Authors are not paid for articles in academic journals but are rewarded instead with fame and adulation.[60]

JPG / JPEG (Joint Photographic Experts Group)

An image format for photographs. Its compression algorithm is 'lossy', so it can generate unwanted artefacts, like speckling, around high-contrast areas. To prevent this, use **PNG** for lettering and line drawings.

Justified

Text that has a neat edge on both sides. This is accomplished by adding extra space between words. If the layout has short lines of text, such as next to images or in newspaper columns, this can result in unsightly **Rivers** of whitespace.

---

[60] Or what passes for fame within their specific fields; academics don't usually make it to the Oscars.

K

KDP (Kindle Direct Publishing)
Part of Amazon, and the world's biggest **Indie Publisher**, both of **eBooks** and paperbacks. KDP paid out over $300 million in **Royalties** in 2019. Recently, KDP added hardbacks to its capabilities.

Kerning
The space between successive characters. This is normally automatically adjusted, but some **Display Typefaces** may not cope well with words such as SAVINGS, where the A and V should overlap to avoid a large gap.

Keyword
A word or short phrase that will enable readers to find your work. Keywords are important for search engine optimisation (**SEO**) and for online writing websites such as Wattpad. On Amazon, the keywords you choose for your book determine which subcategories it is listed in.

You do not need to repeat the words from your title, as those will already be indexed. Instead, think of words that someone might use when looking for your book on Google.

L

Landscape
An image or page having an **Aspect Ratio** wider than tall. The converse is **Portrait**.

Layout
Arranging text, images and design features to form pleasing and consistent pages.

Lead (say leed, not led)
The first paragraph of an article. Many readers (including prospective publishers) will read only this, so it should convey the topic succinctly and draw the reader in.

Leading (say ledding, not leeding)
Early printing used letters moulded in lead blocks of a uniform **Point** height. To give the printed pages a more open look, thin strips of lead were laid between successive rows of text. This is the leading. 12/14 means 12pt text with a 2pt lead strip between giving an overall height of 14pts.

Word processors use **Line Spacing** instead, with the default of 1.15 giving the close equivalent of 12/13.8 leading.

Line Editing
See **Copy Editing**.

Line Spacing
The ratio of space between successive baselines to the height of the text. Many word processors use a default of 1.15, meaning that the space is 15% of the **Point Size**.

Scripts and academic papers often require double spacing to facilitate **Mark-Up**.

List Price
Also called RRP or cover price. The nominal price, which may be on the barcode or printed on the cover.

Literary Agent
See **Agent**.

Logline
A summary of your story, similar to an **Elevator Pitch**, but even shorter.

Using the classic structure of [protagonist] + [inciting event] + [quest] + [problem], a logline for *Back to the Future* might be:

> *Marty McFly is accidentally sent into his parent's past by an eccentric scientist. Now they must fix time before the future disappears.*

Not to be confused with a **Strapline / Tagline**, which is a snappy slogan.

> *Marty McFly broke time. He's got one week to fix it.*

Lowercase
Also called **Minuscules**.

When printing involved actual pieces of lead type, these were stored in cabinets, with the capital letters of each **Font** stored in a drawer above their corresponding small letters. The letters in the top drawer became known as **Uppercase** letters and the ones in the bottom as lowercase.

M

Mailing List

An important way to build your readership. Many **Blogs** and **Websites** allow visitors to sign up and have your golden globs of wisdom drop straight into their mailbox each week.

You need to steer a fine line between posting often enough to generate momentum, and spamming your readers. Every day is probably too much, every month is too little.

Majuscules

Another name for capitals or **Uppercase** letters. The opposite of **Minusculus**.

Manuscript

Your writing before it is published.

Mark-Up

Annotating **Copy** to note corrections, and to mark parts to be added or removed. (See killing your **Darlings**.) Traditionally, mark-up was done with a **Blue Pencil**.

Minuscules

Another name for small or **Lowercase** letters. The opposite of **Majuscules**.

Mobi

A file format for **eBooks** (extension .MOB) that can be read on many types of **eReader**. Other formats are **ePub** and **PDF**.

Mobi files can include **DRM** information to prevent the book from being copied.

N

Narrative Arc
Also called a story arc, this is the order of events in your novel. The basic structure of most plots is like a mountain. In the foothills, we meet the characters and plant the seeds of the later conflict. Then comes the 'inciting incident', the event that boots someone up the backside and makes the story happen – Romeo spots Juliet at a party, Katniss volunteers in place of her sister.

We climb the slope as the hero faces increasing difficulties and at the peak of the mountain we come to the climax – the hero is in mortal danger or struggling with some dreadful moral dilemma.

On the way down, the problem is resolved, the hero learns a valuable lesson and emerges a better person. And at base camp on the far side, we tie up the loose ends.[61]

Niche
A limited market for a specific interest. Readers in a niche may be few, but they are very engaged.

Non-breaking Space
Used in **Typesetting** to make sure that successive words are not separated over a line break. For example, 50 mph might be given a non-breaking space to prevent it being rendered as 50 mph.

---

[61] In Gilbert and Sullivan operettas, the reformed pirates marry the professional bridesmaids. In Shakespeare tragedies, everyone dies.

O

Op-Ed
A weighty article that appears opposite the editorial page of a newspaper or serious magazine.

Orphans
See **Widows and Orphans**.

Other Publications
A page at the back of a book listing titles by the same author, often with a **Tagline** or **Logline**. In **eBooks**, it has hyperlinks to the books on an online bookseller or the author's **Website**.

Out of Print
A book that is no longer being printed and is only available second-hand. With the advent of **eBooks,** there is debate as to whether a book is considered out of print when only eBooks are available.

Oxford Comma
Also called the serial comma, this is a comma preceding the final element in a list. Some **Style Guides** declare it anathema, while others (such as the Oxford **University Press** and many US guides) recommend its use.

Personally, I use an Oxford comma where one is needed for clarity and omit it elsewhere.

For example: *Here is a photo of my parents, the Pope and Michelle Obama.* I prefer: *Here is a photo of my parents, the Pope, and Michelle Obama.*[62]

---

[62] Phew!

P

Pantone / PMS
A way of specifying colours via the Pantone Matching System (PMS). Ikea Yellow is PMS 115 C.

PDF (Portable Document Format)
A document format that cannot easily be altered. PDFs are used for **Proofs**, for uploading books to **Indie Publishing** services and for reading books on **eReaders**.

Peer-Review
The means by which academic writing is scrutinised by fellow academics before being published in a **Journal**.

Pen Name
A pseudonym used for writing. Some authors use pen names for different **Genres**.

The awesome Ronnie Barker wrote sketches as Gerald Wiley because he wanted them to stand on their own merit and not because of his name.

Periodical
A publication that appears regularly, such as a newspaper, magazine or **Journal**, and as opposed to a single-issue book.

Perspective
The viewpoint of the story and whether it tells the reader about what I do (first person), what you do (second person) or what he or she does (third person).

Non-fiction instruction books (such as this) are often written in the second person; fiction is usually in the first or third.

Here are the starts of three books written from different perspectives:

- I returned from the City about three o'clock on that May afternoon pretty well disgusted with life. I had been three months in the Old Country, and was fed up with it.
  — *The Thirty-Nine Steps, John Buchan*
- You are not the kind of guy who would be at a place like this at this time of the morning. But here you are, and you cannot say that the terrain is entirely unfamiliar.
  — *Bright Lights, Big City, Jay McInerney*
- Once upon a time, there was a frog called Mr. Jeremy Fisher; he lived in a little damp house amongst the buttercups at the edge of a pond.
  — *Jeremy Fisher, Beatrix Potter*

Pitch

Also called a query letter, this is the most important part of a **Proposal** or **Submission**. A good pitch is no more than a few hundred words long and tells the publisher *what* your book is, *why* people would want to read it and *who* those people are. The **Synopsis** of the plot includes spoilers – the publisher wants to know how it ends!

You can also include credentials such as your existing fanbase, previous publishing success and (where appropriate) your qualifications for writing on that topic. Mention successful books that are similar and note why yours is different (its **USP**).

Pixel

Short for pic__ture el__ement, a pixel is one of the millions of dots of which digital images are composed. Each pixel contains the colour information for that dot in either **CMYK** or **RGB** format.

Plagiarism
Using words or ideas from other works without attribution or permission. This is a grave offence in academic circles and can run you foul of **Copyright** laws in any genre. Use **References** to avoid charges of plagiarism and if in doubt, attribute!

Portrait
An image or page having an **Aspect Ratio** taller than wide. The converse is **Landscape**.

PNG (Portable Network Graphic)
An image format that has lossless compression, making it better than **JPG** but at the expense of larger file size. PNG images can also have transparent backgrounds.

POD (Print-on-Demand)
A modern method of book production that has enabled the **Indie Publishing** revolution. Books are printed only when they are purchased, meaning that publishers do not have the financial risk of printing hundreds of books that may not sell. Many **Traditional Publishers** now use POD technology.

Point / Point Size
A unit of measurement used in **Typesetting**. There are 72 points in an inch, so a 36pt font measures approximately ½" from the top of an **Ascender** to the bottom of a **Descender**.

POV (Point of View)
See **Perspective**.

Preface
An introduction to a book written by the author from outside the text. This is different from a **Foreword** (not by the author) or **Introduction** (from within the text).

Pre-Orders

Books ordered before **Publication Date**. A large number of pre-orders can help to push a book up the bestsellers list.

Print Ready

The final version of the book, after the **Proofs** have been checked and the book is ready to be sent to the printer. For digital printing, this will usually be in a **PDF** file format with **Embedded Fonts**.

Print Run

The number of books printed at one time. Before digital printing, this had to be a large number because of the time taken to set up each page. Modern **Print-on-Demand** services usually have a print run of one.

Proposal

But, dearest, we hardly know each other.
Oh, not that sort of ... ahem ... sorry. I'll start again.

Also called a submission. This is the package that you would send to an **Agent** or publisher. The **Submission Guidelines** tell you what to include, but it is typically a **Query Letter** or **Pitch**, a one-page **Synopsis** and sample chapters.

You should also state the **Target Audience**, and **Genre** of your book, such as fantasy, literary fiction, chick-lit, crime, sci-fi, children's and young adult.

Proofs

The pre-print version of your book or article so that you can make one final check for errors in **Layout**, page numbering, **Alignment** etc. Usually in **PDF**.

Proof Reading

The final check of **Proofs** before the book or article goes to print. Not the same as **Copy Editing**, which is the stage before.

It's almost impossible to proof read your own work because you will see what you expect. Get someone else to do it, and don't be surprised to find errors even if the writing has been checked several times before.

Pseudonym
See **Pen Name**.

Publication Date
The date from which your book is available to purchase. You can promote your book beforehand to generate **Pre-Orders**.

Publicity Tour
See Book Tour.

Publishing Services
See **Author Services**.

Publishing House
A company that turns **Manuscripts** into books, magazines, **Journals**, newspapers etc. They may be **Traditional Publishers** or **Hybrid**. The majority of books published in the English-speaking world are produced by **The Big Five/Four** or one of their many **Imprints**.

Pull Quote
A short, attention-grabbing quotation from the text, often set out in a box or a larger font as a layout feature.

Not the same as a **Block Quote,** which is a way of setting out a longer quotation as an indented block within the main text.

Q

Query Letter
See **Pitch**.

Quarto

Back in the days of letterpress printing, the easiest way to make a book was to print on a sheet of paper, both sides, then fold it in half to make two leaves of four pages. You could put several of those together to produce a slim book with large pages. This was called a folio (from the Latin for 'leaf') such as Shakespeare's first folio.

If you folded the paper twice, into quarters, you would produce a smaller book with twice as many pages, a quarto. Fold again and you get octavo.

Although the final book size depends on the size of paper you started with, quarto is still used to refer to large-format books approximately 10" x 8" (25cm x 20cm).

You don't really need to know this, but it's a fun word and without it, the entry for Q would be very small.

R

Recto
The right-hand page of a book. Important parts, such as the **Contents**, **Dedication** or a new chapter, are usually on this page. The opposite is **Verso**.

References
The list of books and other sources that you have quoted from, alluded to, or which have influenced your thinking. For certain types of writing, **Academic Referencing** is important to avoid **Plagiarism**, a most serious offence.

Rejection Slips
Standardised responses to a **Submission** saying, "Thanks, but no thanks."

Try not to take rejections personally. They do not mean that your manuscript is bad, only that it does not fit that **Publishing House**'s portfolio at that time. J. K. Rowling received nearly a dozen rejection slips before she found a publisher for *Harry Potter*. Mere mortals like us can expect to collect far more.

Resolution
Image quality expressed in dots per inch (**DPI**). Resolution depends on the number of **Pixels** in the original image and the size at which the image is reproduced. Most printing requires a minimum of 300dpi.

Screens have a lower resolution than printers so images in eBooks can have fewer pixels than in print books, reducing storage and transmission requirements. They can also be full-colour at no additional cost.

Returns
Unsold books sent back to the publisher for a full refund. Bookshops usually only take books on a **Sale-or-Return** basis.

Review Copy
See **Advanced Copy**.

RGB (Red Green Blue)
A way of describing a colour by the proportions of red, green and blue light. The amounts of each colour can be specified in decimal numbers from 0 to 255 or hexadecimal (base 16) from 0 to FF preceded by a #. Ikea Yellow is 255, 218, 26 or #FFDA1A.

RGB is used by computer monitors which are mixing light, whereas printers use **CMYK** because they are mixing inks.

Rights
The ways that a publisher can use your **Manuscript**. Forms include volume rights, serial rights, translation rights, reprint rights, exclusive and non-exclusive rights.

Rivers
Apparent lines of whitespace running through a page of text. They are caused when gaps between words accidentally align.

Roman
The standard form of a typeface, as opposed to *italic* or **bold**.

Royalties
The percentage of a book's sale price paid to the author, which can vary from 5% to 70%. Royalties are specified in a publishing **Contract**, and established authors might receive an **Advance**.

RRP (Recommended Retail Price)
See **List Price**.

S

Sale-or-Return
Placing books with a bookseller on the understanding that you (the author or publisher) will take them back for a full refund if they do not sell within a certain period (**Shelf Life**).

Self-Publishing
Any of the methods of publishing which are organised by the author, rather than a **Publishing House**.

Some people use self-publishing as a term of disdain, equating it with the **Vanity Press**. However, there are many reputable options these days, and self-publishing is a viable route for respected authors.

Flavours include **Indie Publishing**, in which the author takes full responsibility for all aspects of publication and **Hybrid**, where the author and publisher share risks and profits.

SEO (Search Engine Optimization)
Using appropriate **Keywords** to lift your **Website**, book or **Blog** higher in search rankings.

Serial Comma
See **Oxford Comma**.

Serialised Fiction
Publishing a story one chapter at a time, either in print magazines or on social publishing websites. Sherlock Holmes started life as serialised fiction.[63]

---

[63] The original one, not Benedict Whatsisname.

Shelf Life

How long a book will stay on shelves before being sent back to the publisher as a **Return**.

Slush Pile

Unsolicited manuscripts that used to end up on a literal pile by an editor's desk. These days the pile is more often electronic.

As an encouraging anecdote, consider that even *Harry Potter* ended up in a slush pile until an editor gave it to his 8-year-old daughter to read:

"She came down from her room an hour later glowing," reported Nigel Newton. "She nagged and nagged me in the following months, wanting to see what came next."

Bloomsbury bought the rights to the manuscript for £2,500, and what happened next is modern history.

Soft Hyphen

An optional hyphen placed in a word to ensure that the line break (if required) comes at a suitable place.

SPaG (Spelling, Punctuation and Grammar)

What it says on the tin.

Your story may be of a noble, timeless theme that rises above such mundanities as how many 'c's in necessary,[64] and whether the full stop goes inside or outside the speech marks,[65] but no-one will want to read your wonderful words if the manuscript looks like it was written by a gibbon.[66]

---

[64] One.

[65] Inside.

[66] With apologies to gibbons.

Speculative / Speculative Fiction

a) A manuscript sent to a publisher without invitation. A synonym for **Unsolicited** and the opposite of **Commissioned**. Speculative manuscripts land in the **Slush Pile**, to be read when the **Acquisitions Editor** has time. If a publisher says they do not accept unsolicited manuscripts, don't send one.

b) Speculative Fiction is a collection of **Genres** featuring elements that do not exist in reality. It includes supernatural, futuristic, time-travel, alternative history, superheroes and conventional sci-fi. This is a hugely popular area of fiction.

Stet

Markup counteracting any previous corrections, retaining the original version. In other words, "Sorry, just ignore me."

Story Arc

See **Narrative Arc**.

Strapline

Also called a tagline, this is a catchphrase for your book – what you'd put on the movie posters, should your book ever make it that far.

It's shorter than a **Logline** (a one-sentence summary), or an **Elevator Pitch** (two or three sentences).

Structural Editing

See **Content Editing**.

Style Guide

The conventions of **SPaG** that a magazine, **Journal** or multi-authored book uses. Guides cover items such as how to punctuate direct speech, subhead capitalisations, and whether or not to use the **Oxford Comma** (note use of Oxford comma).

A style guide give the publication a consistent look across all authors, so follow the conventions or risk irritating your editor!

Popular style guides include:

- UK: Guardian, Cambridge, MHRA (Modern Humanities Referencing Association, mostly academic)
- US: Chicago, AP (Associated Press, mostly **Periodicals**), Harvard

Submission
See **Proposal**.

Submission Guidelines
A **Publishing House**'s rules on how to submit **Manuscripts**. You must follow these to the tiniest speck of ink on each letter. If they say no **Unsolicited** manuscripts, don't send one. If they say submit between certain dates, do. If they say send a one-page **Query Letter** and two sample chapters, send exactly that.

Synopsis
This is part of your **Query Letter** or **Pitch** to a publisher or **Agent**. For fiction, it should comprise descriptions of your main characters and settings, and a summary of the plot's **Narrative Arc** including the ending.

Synopses are usually written in the third person, present tense and are somewhere around 500 words, but consult the **Submission Guidelines** for details. You may want to write several synopses for different audiences.

T

Tagline
See **Strapline**.

Target Audience
The groups of people who are most likely to buy the book. It is a good idea to identify your target audience before you start writing, and to keep them in mind throughout.

Be as specific as possible in your **Pitch**. No editor wants to hear, "This book is for everyone." That simply means you haven't thought about your target audience enough.

Template
A standard page **Layout** with set **Margins**, **Gutter** and heading styles. Many **Indie Publishing** platforms supply templates for common **Trim Sizes**.

Thumbnail
A small version of an image, often 50 or 100px tall, employed in online bookshop listings. Make sure that your **Cover Image** works at thumbnail size.

Title Page
The first page of your **Front Matter**. Simply repeats the information from the cover: title, subtitle and author.

TOC (Table of Contents)
See **Contents**.

Tone
The style of writing – chatty, scholarly, dramatic, funny etc. **Line Editing** checks that the tone suits the intended **Audience**.

Traditional Publisher

A company that buys the rights to publish your book. It takes on the associated financial risk and sees the book through to final distribution in bookshops, libraries and online, paying **Royalties** on books sold.

Most print books are produced by **The Big Five/Four** or one of their **Imprints**, but there are also myriad smaller publishers often specialising in **Niche** markets.

Beware of a publisher who is overly enthusiastic about your manuscript, especially if submission fees are mentioned – **Vanity Presses** like to masquerade as traditional publishing houses.

Trim Size

The final dimensions of a book, frequently given in inches. Popular trim sizes vary by **Genre**, with fiction usually between 5x8 and 6x9. Non-fiction books can be a little bigger, up to 7x10, while textbooks and children's books can be as big as 8½x11.

Typeface

The style of lettering, eg Calibri or Arial. The combination of typeface, **Point Size** and **Variation** is called a **Font**.

Typesetting

Originally this meant setting individual pieces of lead type into frames, but now a synonym of **Layout**. it is done on computers via **DTP** (desk-top publishing) programs.

U

University Presses
For example, OUP, Oxford University Press. These are owned and run by established universities and publish academic and scholarly titles.

Unsolicited
See **Speculative**.

Uppercase
Also called **Majuscules**.

When printing involved actual pieces of lead type, these were stored in cabinets, with the capital letters stored in a drawer above their corresponding small letters. The letters in the bottom drawer became known as **Lowercase** letters and the ones in the top as uppercase.

URL (Uniform Resource Locator)
See **Domain Name**.

USP (Unique Selling Point)
This is what makes your book unique and marketable. Make sure you emphasise this in your **Elevator Pitch** and **Query Letter**.

V

Vanity Press / Publishers
A pejorative term for **Self-Publishing**.

More accurately, it refers to companies that make their profits from the author, not from the books. You can distinguish these from legitimate small **Traditional Publishers** when you see adverts guaranteeing to print your book, with no editorial oversight, and charging you three arms, two legs and a torso.

Variations
The different styles of a **Typeface**, eg *italic*, **bold**, Roman (normal) or ^{superscript}. The combination of typeface, variation and **Point Size** comprise a **Font**.

Verso
The left-hand page of a book, as opposed to **Recto**. The less-than-thrilling parts of your book, such as the **Copyright Page** would normally appear here.

Virtual Book Tour
Like a normal **Book Tour** but online, consisting of webinars, **Blog Tours**, giveaways and interviews. Has the advantage that it can easily be international, but the disadvantage[67] that you cannot meet actual people.

Voice
See **Tone**.

---

[67] Whether this counts as a disadvantage depends on your troglodyte tendencies, of course.

W

Website

A great place to meet your readers and display your **Backlist**. You might have a static website that tells readers about you, gives information about (and possibly sells) your books, allows people to book you as a speaker, etc., or you could have a regularly updated **Blog** and associated **Mailing List**.

See also **Domain Name**.

Whitespace

The space on a page, around images, above and below titles etc. This gives the page its 'feel' – cramped and heavy or spacious and airy. If in doubt, add more.

Whitespace also refers to inadvertent patches of white caused by awkwardly justified text. The extra spaces added between words to make lines the same length can produce **Rivers** of whitespace. You can avoid these by making the lines longer, the text smaller, changing the typeface or inserting a **Soft Hyphen** in one of the earlier lines. This can reflow the entire paragraph and blast that pesky river to smithereens.

Wholesale Discount

The discount from **List Price** that wholesalers and bookshops get. Typically 55%.

Widows and Orphans

These are single lines that sit alone at the top (widow) or bottom (orphan) of a page, with the rest of the paragraph on the previous or following page. Both are the result of poor **Layout** and should be detected at the **Proof Reading** stage. You must ruthlessly eliminate all widows and orphans!

Word Count
The number of words in a book, article or other written piece. If you are given a word count, stick to it. Poetry may have a line count instead.

Academic writing handed in for marking does not usually include **Appendices**, **References** or **Bibliography** in the word count because these are not part of the student's work, but non-fiction works and papers for **Journals** usually do because these still take up room in a book.

Work-for-Hire
A flat fee for your work instead of **Royalties**. This often applies to **Commissioned** shorter pieces such as specialist chapters or articles, rather than **Speculative** manuscripts.

X, Y, Z

Ummn ...[68]

Xenophon[69], Yttrium[70] and Zagreb[71]?

---

[68] My estimable editor points out that I could usefully include 'x-height, the height of a lower-case letter x'. But that would kinda spoil the joke, don't you think?

[69] Xenophon was a Greek philosopher. (Weren't they all?)

[70] Yttrium is element number 39.

[71] Zagreb is the capital of Croatia.

The Stuff at the Back

Technically the **Back Matter**, but you knew that already.[72]

---

[72] Oh, come on. You've finished the book. No one reads this stuff unless they're procrastinating. You're not procrastinating, are you? No? Good. Then get your writing off your hard disk and into hard copy. What are you waiting for, the credits?

Useful Websites and Organisations

These suggestions are not exhaustive, I've not necessarily used all of them personally, and I'm not endorsing them. They're simply places for you to start your search.

ACX
Audiobook Creation Exchange. Amazon's audiobook platform, distributing through iTunes and Amazon's Audible.

The Alliance of Independent Authors
Group for indie authors with many member benefits.

Apple Books for Authors
Ummn, it's the Apple books site for authors.

Authors Publish
Newsletter of publishers and advice from Writer's Workshop.

Book Baby
Self-publishing services including editing, formatting, cover design, print-on-demand and marketing.

Book Cover Zone
Custom and pre-made book covers.

CIEP
The Chartered Institute of Editors and Proofreaders. Training courses and directory of author services.

The Cover Collection
Custom and pre-made book covers.

Draft 2 Digital
Distributor for indie-published eBooks, with free ISBNs.

IngramSpark
Print-on-demand publisher and wholesaler for hardbacks, paperbacks and eBooks.

KDP
Kindle Direct Publishing. Amazon's print-on-demand platform for paperbacks, hardbacks and eBooks.

Kobo
eBook publishing platform via Kobo Writing Life.

National Association of Writers and Groups
Umbrella organisation for UK writers, with editorial services, courses and competitions.

Self Publishing Advice
Free advice from the Alliance of Independent Authors.

Smashwords
Distributor of indie eBooks to readers, retailers and libraries.

The Society of Authors
Advice, news and events and special-interest groups.

Taylor and Francis
Umbrella publisher of a vast range of academic journals with plenty of help for those navigating the publishing swamp.

Writers and Artists
Producers of an annual book of publishers and author services, plus an informative website.

Further Reading

The best way to improve your writing is to write.[73]

The second-best way to improve your writing is to read good writing. A great excuse for a cake and coffee, too. (If you're reading, it counts work. Honest.)

The third-best way is to read *about* good writing.

If you'd like advice from world-class authors, top editors and others who know what they're talking about, here are some books about the craft of writing. They're mostly focussed on fiction, but some apply to non-fiction as well. Some I own, some are recommendations from others.

Top of the list, and highly recommended even if you don't like his fiction genre, is Stephen King.

On Writing
Stephen King

Part memoir, part masterclass by one of the bestselling authors of all time, this superb volume is a revealing and practical view of the writer's craft, comprising the basic tools of the trade every writer must have. Brilliantly structured, friendly and inspiring.

This is the source of the 'kill your darlings' quote - brilliant (if slightly gory!)

---

[73] Just get on with it. Bum on seat. Write. Doesn't matter how good or bad it is. Bad writing can always be improved; non-existent writing cannot. Just write. Then, when you've finished, edit. And edit some more. And more. See footnote 1.

Save the Cat! Writes a Novel
Jessica Brody

You can apply the famed 'Save the Cat!'[74] methodology to the world of novel writing with 15 way-points to guide your story to a thrilling climax. With detailed analyses of successful stories and quirky, original insights, you can craft a plot that will captivate – and a novel that will sell.

I find these way-points very useful for crafting a narrative arc, and there are plenty of hints for chasing your hero up a tree and then throwing stones at them. Highly recommended.

Are You Actually Going to Write a Book or Just Talk About It?
Brandon Q. Scott

Do you have a story in your head that won't go away? Well, isn't it about time you did something about that?

Reviewer: *This book is a really motivating and easy read. It is the best purchase I've ever made. After only 10 pages I put the book down and started writing.*

Plot Perfect
Paula Munier

This plotting primer reveals the secrets of creating a story structure that works no matter what your genre. Filled with writing exercises, plotting templates, and expert advice, *Plot Perfect* helps you dive into the intricacies of plotting and write a compelling story that readers won't be able to resist.

---

[74] 'Saving the Cat' refers to a plot device where a rough diamond (later, the hero) rescues a cat. Preferably one belonging to a little girl. With pigtails. (The girl, not the cat.)

Editing Secrets of Best-Selling Authors
Kathy Ide

In this book, you'll find a wealth of suggestions from authors who have studied editing techniques and implemented them in their books. If you're an aspiring, beginning, or intermediate writer, this book will help you polish your manuscript and get it ready for publication.

The Author's Toolkit
Mary Embree

All writers yearn for success and recognition. And now we are entering a golden era in which self-publishers are in the driver's seat. Aspiring authors, students, and even established writers will find the resources they need to achieve their goals and avoid common writer pitfalls.

How to Write Dazzling Dialogue
James Scott Bell

You may know the fundamentals of how to write fiction. You may be more than competent in plot, structure and characters. But if your dialogue is dull, it will drag the whole story down. On the other hand, dialogue that is crisp and full of tension immediately grabs the reader.

How to Write and Sell Great Short Stories
Linda M. James

Do you know: How to create characters who are more real than your family and friends? How to create vivid locations that readers can actually see? How to create such intriguing plots that readers are desperate to carry on reading? You don't? Then you need to buy this invaluable book.

Writing the Cozy Mystery
Nancy J. Cohen

Do you want to write a mystery but don't have a clue where to start? With chapters including The Muddle in the Middle, Romance and Murder, Special Considerations for Cozy Writers, Keeping a Series Fresh, Writing the Smart Synopsis, Mystery Movies, and Marketing Tips.

The Guide to Writing Fantasy and Science Fiction
Philip Athans

Create worlds that draw your readers in and keep them reading and learn how to prepare your work for today's market. From devising clever plots and building complex characters to inventing original technologies, find all you need to write strong, saleable narratives.

Writing Book Blurbs and Synopses
Rayne Hall

Do you want a synopsis that persuades agents to request the whole manuscript? This guide shows you step-by-step how to create six effective short forms for selling your manuscript to publishers and readers, including synopsis, pitch, blurb and tagline.

Self-Editing for Fiction Writers
Renni Browne and Dave King

Hundreds of books have been written on the art of writing. Here, at last, is a book by two professional editors to teach writers the techniques of editing that turn promising manuscripts into published novels and short stories.

About the Author

Hi, I'm Fay.

Here I am, signing a book in one of my favourite places, the library of my college in Cambridge. (I'm not writing in a library book, honest.)

In no particular order, I am a knitologist, mathematician, mum, author, teacher, tea-bibber, geek, blogger, theology researcher and Trekkie.

I have been involved in publishing, both doing it and teaching it, since the late 1980s, covering aspects from writing to proof reading via copy-editing and layout.

I have solo-authored six books in addition to this one, several of which have topped their respective charts on Amazon. I am a contributory author to four more books, some indie-published, some traditional. I also write a popular weekly blog, The Reflectionary, and have published papers in academic journals.

When not writing, I teach maths for a living and spend most of the rest of the time being creative. I live with my children and pet dragon in the English Midlands in a house full of glue sticks and mess (which I blame on the kids, but really, it's me).

Fay

Other Publications

A Bucketful of Ideas for Church Drama

"Parables as Jesus would have told them – witty and thought-provoking."

#1 Best-Seller in Puppet Scripts!

"Thirty Pieces of Chocolate is a fine pun-run."

A(nother) Bucketful of Ideas for Church Drama

14 scripts including CRISP-tingle, a pop-up nativity, and lots more.

"Delivers the timeless truths of scripture in a modern and punchy manner."

God Is With Us – Everywhere!

Featuring a cool Gabriel, terrified shepherds and three confused scientists, this witty yet poignant Nativity is perfect for your school or church production.

"Thank you for your script, we had it at our online carol service yesterday - and it went down a storm!"

#1 Best-Seller in Christian Youth Ministry!

Walking to Bethlehem

Twenty-five imaginative devotions for adults and children, with reflective colouring and craft ideas.

"Travel from BC to AD to focus your mind on the road to Bethlehem. Fun and devotional, practical and creative."

#1 Best-Seller in Advent Devotions!

The Big Story

Discover the Bible as one big story of God and God's people, from the very beginning of everything up to the wonder of Easter.

#1 Best-Seller in Bible Meditations!

Perfect for personal devotions, for weekly Bible studies and youth groups, discover The Big Story today.

Broken Bits & Weirdness

Meet nine of the Bible's dismal failures and learn how God still loves them (and us), even with our Broken Bits & Weirdness.

With Bible notes, crafts, cooking, colouring and other resources, and studies for Good Friday and Easter Day, this is perfect for Lent or any time of year.

#1 Best-Seller in Bible Meditations!

Creativity Matters

Join thirteen authors as they share their passion for why you should write in their genre and find your own passion as you read.

In my chapter, 'Why Write Drama?', you can discover what makes drama sparkle, and why you shouldn't take your gran to see a Greek satyr play!

URC Prayer Handbooks

I have been a commissioned author for the URC's prayer handbooks for several years.

They are full of original, passionate, quirky and relevant prayers, this year focussing on a theme of 'Freed to Live!'

Each Sunday has several prayers linked to readings from the Revised Common Lectionary. They are suitable for both congregational and private use, using contemporary language and covering a broad range of topics.

You can buy the most recent prayer handbooks at the URC's website shop.

www.ingramcontent.com/pod-product-compliance
Lightning Source LLC
Chambersburg PA
CBHW071518080526
44588CB00011B/1476